HURRY UP *and* WAIT

Dianne Collier

An Inside Look at Life as a Canadian Military Wife

Dianne Collier

Published by

Creative Bound Inc.
P.O. Box 424
151 Tansley Drive
Carp, Ontario
Canada K0A 1L0

Tel: (613) 831-3641
Fax: (613) 831-3643

ISBN 0-921165-34-X
Printed and bound in Canada

Book design by Wendelina O'Keefe
    Cover illustration by Brock Nicol
    Cartoons by Sophie Patenaude, The Joy of Motherhood
    Cartoons, chapters 2 and 8, by Dave Doran

Canadian Cataloguing in Publication Data

Collier, Dianne
        Hurry up & wait : an inside look at life as a Canadian military wife

ISBN 0-921165-34-X

        1. Military spouses—Canada. 2. Canada.
Canadian Army—Military life.   I. Title.

U773.C65 1994   355.1'0971   C94-900170-8

1st printing, May 1994
2nd printing, November 1994

Dedication

To a very special Engineer, my husband John, who proved that a positive attitude, determination and perseverance, when applied against insurmountable obstacles, will see you emerge the victor! And to my sons Chris and Trevor who, because of this lifestyle, have grown into self-assured, intelligent, well-rounded, independent young men.

I'm extremely proud of them all.

❋   ❋   ❋

This book is also dedicated to all you military wives who have 'hung in there' through the bad times as well as the good.

We've all heard the saying "Behind every successful man is a woman!" Well, in the military community there is a strong feeling that for every medal hubby receives his wife has earned two!

It is my sincere wish that every one of you military men who read this book will see your wife in a new light and recognize her for the jewel that she is. May I suggest that you re-confirm your love for her by acknowledging her commitment to you with a beautiful, long-stemmed rose? Isn't it time to tell her what a special lady she is?

Contents

Foreword

We (husbands) don't do it on purpose! It just seems natural to exaggerate a 'little' as we explain the difficulties of military married life to our prospective wives. Unfortunately, we do such a good job of highlighting the perils that our captive audience decides that we are merely trying to enhance our macho image and they usually ignore us—particularly when we launch into the bit about having to put our profession before family. We take their indifference as consent and end up condemning ourselves to a lifetime of "But, I warned you it was going to be like this, honey!", as we bring home word of yet another posting, exercise, course or UN mission.

As the general officer who was made responsible for developing the policies to integrate women into the combat trades of the Canadian Forces, I get a certain satisfaction from the fact that well over two thousand service women now have to convince their husbands that occasionally Dad and the kids will come in second to Mom's professional obligations. But that's another story; this book is about the wives and kids who make it possible for Dad to serve their country and carry out the wishes of the government of the day.

When I first spoke to Dianne about the book, I erroneously assumed she was working on a manual of instructions for wives of Canadian servicemen. My wife had been given an American version of such a book as a joke just before I took command of my battalion in 1977; I got the message when she relegated it to the garbage disposal. Needless to say, I was a bit concerned that Dianne's book would suffer a similar fate if it tried to preach on the role of the military wife.

I was pleasantly surprised when I read Dianne's first draft. This book doesn't preach. It is a delightful collection of anecdotes, survey results and sage advice from wives and kids of all ages who have been there. Anyone who has spent time in the military or married to it will find themselves with a kink in their neck from all the nodding in agreement after a few hours of reading. In many cases only the places and names have to be changed to match personal experiences.

It is not all good news; far from it. There are stories and comments from those who have not enjoyed their families' association with the Profession of Arms. Not everyone is cut out for a nomadic existence marked by frequent periods of extended absences. If you fall into this category, avoid getting involved with anyone wearing a Canadian Forces uniform.

For the relatively new wife—sorry, it's too late to back out, so read on and take solace from the fact that many before you have survived with their sense of humour and sanity intact. Realizing that you are not alone in facing the somewhat bizarre life of a service wife will hopefully make it just a little more tolerable on the bad days.

Without a doubt, the overwhelming rewards of service life shine through the words of Dianne and her collaborators—the spouses and the sons and daughters. Service families provide the anchor, the essential link with reality, as servicemen prepare for a mission that we all hope they never have to carry out—to fight and, if necessary, die, in the pursuit of our national interests.

Toronto, Ontario
4 January 1994
Major General (Ret'd) Lewis W. MacKenzie SBStJ, MSC, CD

Preface

Hurry Up and Wait is a contradictory phrase, but it so accurately describes military life from both the service member's and his wife's point of view, that its use as a title for this book, even when the book was only an idea, was inevitable. My husband gently suggested I might be putting the cart before the horse by having a book title before I had decided on its contents! However, one has only to voice this phrase during any military gathering and you will see heads nod in understanding. What does it mean? According to some of the women I posed this question to:

That's the military in general.

The biggest problem as a military wife is the waiting—waiting for postings, waiting for my husband to come home.

It means the men have to do everything today and they don't need it for a month!

My husband is Airborne, and when the unit was supposed to go to the Western Sahara, there was this big rush to get every-thing ready to go. And then the dates kept changing and eventually everything was cancelled. It was an emotional roller coaster.

. . . you know you are being posted, but you don't know when. There is the rush to get your house ready to sell, but then the

waiting for that posting message seems to take forever to come—and you can't put your house up for sale until you have that little piece of paper in your hand.

To me it means the rush to have the house spic and span and his favourite sweets baked, because my husband is finally coming home—only to have his arrival date changed at the last minute!

It seems everything the military does is rush, rush, rush, but then they always seem to sit around and wait for what to do next.

While life as a military wife can be very rewarding, it can also be very frustrating, lonely and depressing. This book tries to instill a chuckle here and there, to put a little more laughter into this often serious atmosphere. Included are a few articles I've written, and many articles and poems by other women, which show that regardless of our husbands' occupations, we do share a common bond.

I was born and brought up in the Navy port of Halifax, Nova Scotia, and seeing Army or Air Force uniforms was as foreign to me as the wheat on the Prairies! It was interesting to discover, though, on doing a family history of pictures for both my family and my husband's several years ago, that 21 relatives served in the military; of these, three were Navy, two Airforce and all the rest Army.

My criteria for a husband, besides the standard rich, handsome, romantic, thoughtful type who would always put me first, were that he would have no dirt under his fingernails and absolutely no tattoos! Marrying a military man was never even a thought. However, when Cupid decides to have a little shooting practice, the 'victims' have no say in the matter! I married the 'boy next door' who by then had joined the Canadian Army as a Field Engineer and who took me on a 26-year journey that showed me so much of a world I had not previously known and who instilled in this 'city girl' a love of nature and the outdoors.

Having grown up a very organized, plan-ahead person, and one who spent all her single life near the sea, marrying an Army man and living 'inland' more often than not took a lot of adjusting. My husband would say, when I was particularly upset at having my well-laid plans altered because of some military obligation, "You'll get used to it!" I may have gotten used to it, but I never could adopt the attitude of taking one day at a time. And so, about 17 years ago, I found myself drowning my sorrows in a cup of coffee with some neighbours outside our permanent married quarters (PMQs). "Someday I'm going to write a book" was uttered more to provide a bit of laughter than to be taken seriously, as we moaned and groaned about our sad lot. But the idea just would not go away, and as time progressed and my understanding of this lifestyle grew, so did the need to write it all down.

In 1986, after I commented to my husband that the "book" would not leave me alone, he suggested that perhaps it was time I stopped thinking about it and started writing!

But how do you write a book; where do you start? Will people take me seriously or will they laugh at the idea?

Well, "That's what friends are for . . ." I decided to test my ideas on my military friends all over Canada and Germany, and be guided by their response. I devised a questionnaire which did not require any names on the response, and bombarded my friends and acquaintances. I felt people would feel more comfortable penning their comments if they did not have to identify themselves. Little did I realize not only how much the women were interested in participating in my project, but how glad they all were that someone was *finally* speaking on their behalf. Not only did they completely fill in the questionnaires, but they sent many letters expressing their thoughts in more detail. Requests to participate in the questionnaire came from all avenues—neighbours, relatives and friends who were military wives—it just snowballed! Two more questionnaires to the wives and one to the teens followed in the ensuing years. These were distributed through various groups and locations on military bases.

Throughout this book I will be referring to these questionnaires and quoting responses. Replies have been received from wives all over Canada and Germany; from Holberg on Vancouver Island to the recruit training base at Cornwallis, Nova Scotia, on to Summerside, P.E.I., and everywhere in between. Their husbands serve in all three elements of the forces (Army, Navy and Air Force), with ranks ranging from Private to Major General. These questionnaires, plus the many, many personal interviews I have conducted, as well as my own writings covering a 'career' of 26 years as a military wife, form the foundation for this book.

Since my home is in Petawawa, Ontario, a large percentage of replies come from this area. However, as Petawawa is home to the

Special Service Force which is tasked with many United Nations missions, Petawawa is not considered your "average" base. Therefore, I felt this was an excellent one on which to centre my comments.

Of all the responses from the wives, the one comment that has continually stayed with me, and one that I have diligently tried to follow, was from my dear friend Cleo, who only asked that I 'tell it like it is.'

I was asked by one lady if I was "qualified" to write a book. If we never attempt anything that we feel we are "not qualified" to do, we will never broaden our horizons or experience the true feeling of accomplishment. I, for one, would probably never have baked a cake if I had first asked myself "am I qualified?"

Names have not been used when quoting interview responses, to protect the identity of those special women who so graciously opened their hearts to me.

Throughout the book I use the term 'military wife' to describe the wife of a service member and not a female serving in the military who is also married.

As military wives we often find ourselves in a position where we must respond or react to situations most wives never face, usually because our husbands are away and therefore we must handle the situation by ourselves. If we stay tucked safely inside our 'cocoon' we will not survive the military lifestyle, nor will we grow as individuals. I do feel that this is one of the advantages we have over our civilian counterparts. The 'pack up and go' life we lead tends to make us more versatile. You install the curtain rods not because you are 'qualified' to do so (although after one or two moves you really are qualified!) but because you don't want to wait weeks or months for hubby to come home to do it for you! Those who live the military lifestyle are a close-knit group who do not open up readily to 'outsiders.' If I had not been a military wife, this book would not have materialized. I found that public notices in local newspapers and bulletin boards for women to contact me if they were interested in my project were not overly successful; military wives were unwilling to 'make the first move.' However, on contacting people individually, I was always met with enthusiasm and a 'Thank God!' when explaining my purpose. Not only were the women interested in what I was doing and anxious to participate, but they just wanted to talk to someone who really understood where they were coming from; often interviews I expected to last an hour lasted several hours. Because I am 'one of them,' the women greeted me with open arms.

I have met many wonderful people and received 100 per cent cooperation from everyone. Those who were initially sceptical about my project soon rallied once they understood what I was trying to do. The women made me feel 'immediately at home,' and I was eager to continue the friendships so quickly established. But that is all part of military life—after a while you learn to assess people quickly and feel an invisible magnet drawing you close to those with whom you share interests. We only have, on the average, two to four years to establish friends and enjoy them before we must leave and start all over.

Throughout this book I have used a few 'gems' whose authors are unknown, and which have been floating around for many years, passed from one military wife to another. Some are creased and wrinkled from being constantly tucked away for safekeeping while moving from pillar to post and hauled out to share with yet another military wife. Others have been framed and hung on the wall not far from a husband's collection of military certificates, tanks, planes and ships. Attempts to find out the authors' identities left me no further ahead. However, the articles are included here in the hopes that if any authors recognize their work, they will appreciate the fact that it was used with the best of intentions and is repeated here for the further enjoyment of many.

There are so many avenues to this lifestyle that it is impossible to cover them all in one book. The task of deciding what to include and what to leave out was very difficult, and I regret that I was not able to use all the information I received. However, after much deliberation, the aims of the book became clear. Only you, the reader, can decide if I have succeeded in reaching them:

- to show the young military wife that she is not alone in some of the frustrations, loneliness and general emotions she is experiencing—they are common to the lifestyle

- to show her what her life will be like, in general terms, if her husband makes the military his career

- to give civilians an inside look at our life on a day-to-day basis so that hopefully they will understand us much better than they do

- to show our husbands that we really are a special breed; to let them see what we deal with while they are gone and how we feel about the lifestyle we have chosen

- most important, to have our husbands appreciate us much more and take us for granted much less.

It is my hope that all who read this book will not only remember our brave men serving all over the world, but will give a 21 gun salute to the military wives who keep the home fires burning. Chimo!

Dianne Collier

Acknowledgements

As with any project of this magnitude, this book would not have materialized without the support and cooperation of many people.

I am thrilled to be able to include Sophie Patenaude's cartoons, which so accurately depict our lifestyle. A military wife and mother, Sophie has a natural talent for taking pen to hand and producing a sketch that is bound to tug at your heartstrings and find you saying to yourself, "Was she in my house when she drew that?" I owe Sophie a debt of gratitude for putting the experiences of many wives into cartoon form and thus creating a 'complete' look to this book.

The interest and encouragement from the military community alone was tremendous. So many women helped in so many ways that their efforts just cannot be measured. You know who you are, ladies; your support will never be forgotten.

A special thank you goes out to the following for their literary contributions:

Leanne Derrah—"Fond Farewells"

Julie A. Doherty—"An Open Letter to My Husband in Namibia"

Linda Gardiner—"Separation (at Its Best)"

Krista Gilby—"Loneliness"

LCol (Ret'd) John Hanson, MSW, CD—Military Family Workshop—"Marrying into the Military"

Lila Hovey—"60 Years as an RCR Wife!"

Marcella Kampman—"Friends Forever: A Moving Experience"

Major W.A. Leavey, CD—"Cyprus Letters"

Carol Nethercott—"Life as a Navy Wife"

Edna Pollock—"Marriage to a Gunner"
Michelle Posthumus—"Deployment"
Barbara Rodler—"Tribute to UN Forces"
Delia Speed—"Eight Weeks Down"

✻   ✻   ✻

A sincere thank you to the following organizations/magazines and individuals for granting permission to reprint the articles indicated:
Military Family Resource Centre—Halifax, Nova Scotia
—"On the Road Again" by Carol Nethercott
—"Western Girl Comes East" by Carol Asbury
—"Time to Take the Quantum Leap" by Crystal G. Mann

Military Family Resource Centre—Esquimalt, British Columbia
—"Posted" by Connie Bowers

Canadian Forces Personnel Newsletter, National Defence Headquarters, Ottawa, Ontario
—Cartoons by Dave Doran; Issue 6/87, 6/88

Sentinel Magazine, National Defence Headquarters, Ottawa, Ontario
—"Crash Course in Survival" by Myrann Nickles, with cartoons by Dave Doran

The Base Post, Petawawa, Ontario
—"Serviceman's Wife—A Very Special Person"

✻   ✻   ✻

1st Battalion, The Royal Canadian Regiment

As any working wife and mother will tell you, trying to find time for yourself after you deal with all your responsibilities can be rather difficult. If your husband is a military man who is constantly away, your spare time can be scarcer than suntan lotion during an Alaskan winter!

My sincere thanks goes out to the 1st Battalion, The Royal Canadian Regiment, in particular to the Commanding Officer, Lieutenant Colonel Mark Skidmore, Deputy Commanding Officer, Major Bob McBride and

Adjutant, Captain Mark Osborne, for their continued interest and encouragement. Their successful efforts in obtaining Regimental funds enabled me to take leave without pay from my job as their secretary to transform a mountain of notes into this book. Besides being a terrific group to work for, The Regiment is tops in my books!

❊ ❊ ❊

A special thank you to the following people for their encouragement and efforts on my behalf:

Mrs. Mia Beno and Brigadier General E.B. Beno, OMM, CD, Commander Special Service Force, Petawawa, Ontario

Mrs. Marilyn Carroll and Chief Petty Officer First Class Jim Carroll, MMM, CD, Canadian Forces Chief Warrant Officer, Ottawa, Ontario

Lieutenant Commander (N) Luce de Montigny, MSW, CD, Regional Social Work Officer Eastern Region, St Hubert, Quebec

Mrs. Donna Eichel and Major General Scott Eichel, CMM, CD, Chief Personnel, Career and Development, Ottawa, Ontario

Captain Don Haisell, CD, former Adjutant of the 1st Battalion, The Royal Canadian Regiment (now serving in the former Yugoslavia)

Major General (Ret'd) Lewis MacKenzie, SBStJ, MSC, CD, Toronto, Ontario

His Worship Mayor Terry McCann, Mayor of Pembroke, Ontario

❊ ❊ ❊

The hat badge shown below is my own personal salute to all my friends in the Canadian Corps of Engineers, who have provided me with so many fond memories and terrific support in times of need.

Military Terms and Definitions

Adjt	Adjutant
APC	Armoured Personnel Carrier
Bug Out	surprise notification of all members of a unit to assemble at a set location as soon as possible
CAF	Canadian Armed Forces
CD	Canadian Decoration (for 12 years service)
2CER	2 Combat Engineer Regiment
Chimo	Eskimo greeting used by Engineers since the 1950s
Civvy	Civilian
CO	Commanding Officer
combats	uniform used for field exercises
coy	Company
CSM	Company Sergeant Major

deuce & 1/2	2 1/2 ton truck
DND	Department of National Defence
dress uniform	uniform used for official functions, parades etc.
Fallex	an exercise held in the Fall of each year
fanout	a reverse pyramid effect where one person calls a pre-determined number of people, each of these people call a specific list of personnel and so on, until every member of the group has been contacted
going to the field	going on an exercise
G-311	building number
Happy Hour	social gathering at the mess—usually held on Fridays
hard rations	dehydrated/boil-in-a-bag rations used in place of fresh food when on a field exercise
HQ	Headquarters
ID	Identification card
interim lodgings	temporary quarters
2IC	Second in command
Jr NCO	Junior Non Commissioned Officer—rank of Private to Master Corporal
MQ	married quarter
MP	military police

mess	building where meals and social functions are held by members of similar rank
March in/out	housing inspection when occupying/leaving married quarters
MWO	Master Warrant Officer
mess kit	uniform worn for formal social functions
MLS	Maple Leaf Services
NDHQ	National Defence Headquarters
OC	Officer Commanding (Company)
O Group	Orders Group—meeting held regularly by leaders to inform subordinates of upcoming plans
Pongo	derogatory term for a member of the Army
Padre	military clergy
pl	platoon
PMQ	permanent married quarter
posting	transferred to a new unit/location
Pte	Private
RP4s	hard rations
RSM	Regimental Sergeant Major
RV 92	Rendezvous 1992—national military exercise
regs	regulations

stop drop	to cancel a parachute descent
stat	immediately
sqn	squadron
UN	United Nations
VCOS	Vice Chief of Staff
WO	Warrant Officer

Chapter 1

A Soldier's Soldier

The *Concise Oxford Dictionary* defines a soldier as "a member of an army" and a wife as "a married woman." It is almost impossible to find a definition of a military wife. We don't ever stay in one place long enough to be properly defined!

To many employers we are a group to avoid—they will just get us trained and we will leave to follow our husbands on their next postings.

To our relatives, we are a vagabond lot whose gypsy-like genes come from who knows where! Our families may have little or no concept of our day-to-day lives, and the extent of their sympathy is often: "Well, you knew that when you married him!"

To the military, we are a necessary, perpetual virus, but great for social functions. (Happily, this attitude is finally changing.) Many wives have concluded that the military's idea of a perfect army is one made up entirely of bachelors!

To each other, we are the ultimate support group—the only ones who can understand what we face day after day.

To our husbands, we are the layer of peanut butter that separates the jam (his military life) from the bread (his home life), and keeps the sandwich together (maintains the family atmosphere even in his absence).

To our children we are the one stable, constant influence in their ever-changing lives—their rock of stability.

A military wife is a soldier's soldier—she is there to serve and assist in any way she can, to make her husband's dedication to his job and his country as smooth-flowing as possible.

Many women have trouble adjusting to life as a military wife, but there are just as many who look on this lifestyle as an adventure. They see themselves as positive partners for their mates, and the anchors of their families. They view each move as a challenge, and an opportunity to learn new skills. Did I say skills? Just take a look at what a soldier's soldier can do:

Jill of All Trades. She can wave her magic rolling pin and turn into a taxi driver, bicycle repair person, carpet shampooer, gourmet cook, furniture arranger or interior decorator. And she can make those curtains from the last PMQ fit the new one even though all the windows are different sizes!

Master's Degree in Responsibility. She can't wait six weeks or months for hubby to come home to decide what to do about Johnny's broken arm or the car muffler lounging on the ground beneath the car.

A Degree in the Science of Moving. She can make 'another move' into a positive, fun-filled experience for her and the kids despite statements like "I'm not moving, I'll run away!" and "Why can't Dad have a *regular job?*" And she can stifle her own tears while she wipes away those in her children's eyes.

Financial Wizard. She must be able to grow money on trees—or else find some way to stretch family finances to cover Joey's hockey registration (he needs new skates again this year), Sara's swimming meets ("You're going on a weekend trip already?") and husband's incidentals for that six-week course (a movie, beer, night out with the boys, a day on the golf course—you know, those diversions necessary to help him relieve the stress of being away from home). She will be expected to have enough left over after paying the bills and the emergency car repairs to "Buy something nice for yourself, honey!" (Don't we wish . . .)

Skill in Single Parenting. She must be willing to raise children almost singlehandedly but be able to graciously relinquish some of this authority to HE THAT VISITS ONCE IN A WHILE.

An Expert in the Social Graces. She'll be saying hello and good-bye time and time again to THE MAN WHO HAS HER HEART and trying not to cry each time. She'll also be saying goodbye to dear friends that she might never see again. And she'll have to be ready to take the first step in her new neighbourhood to make friends.

An Independent Dependant. Even though the military considers her to be a 'dependant' (a label she strongly resents), she'll be on her own for half of most years. Bravery is a welcome ally when she's listening to the strange creaks and groans in each new home when she is trying to sleep—alone again!

Recipe for a Military Housewife

1 1/2 cups patience
1 cup courage
3/4 cup tolerance
Dash of adventure
1 lb. ability

To the above ingredients, add 2 tablespoons elbow grease. Let set alone for 6 months. Marinate frequently with salty tears. Sprinkle ever so lightly with money. Kneed dough until payday. Season with international spices. Bake for 20-25 years or until done. Serve with pride.

Author Unknown

Carol Nethercott, a military wife of 30 years, addressed a military wives' conference in Halifax a few years ago. Her comments echo the thoughts and feelings of many wives.

Condensed from Life as a Navy Wife

by Carol Nethercott

Exactly two months from today, my husband and I will be celebrating our 26th wedding anniversary. That means that for over one half of my life I have been a military wife. Now you would think that after all that time I would have learned what those irritating military abbreviations stand for (such as DGPCO or DDH or VCDS) and that I would have mastered military time. (I still have to ask what 1930 is in 'real' time.) Those things haven't been terribly important to me. What has been important is that I have learned to be relatively successful as a homemaker, home buyer, interior decorator, mother, referee, chauffeur, animal caretaker, financial planner, laundress, seamstress, secretary, repairwoman, career person, friend.

Now nobody believes for a moment that we wake up one morning after the honeymoon is over and are suddenly endowed with all of these abilities. No, it isn't that easy! It takes a lot of hard work and perseverance, particularly as a military wife, because we have had to do it on our own, without the day-to-day support of our spouse. I know; I speak from experience.

I knew my husband exactly seven days when he proposed. I accepted! He sailed for three months, I planned the wedding. We were married three weeks after he returned, had a two-week honeymoon and he sailed for 3 months—and continued to sail for the better part of 18 years. In fact, his first shore posting came 15 years after we were married. When you translate that into days and nights of coping with children, loneliness, running a household and maintaining one's sanity, it is absolutely mind-boggling. When I think back to raising three sons—each exactly two years apart (all September babies, by the way—hubby did manage to be home for the holidays), I remember the six years of always having at least one child in diapers—long before disposable diapers became popular. I remember the long evenings, after the children were put to bed, the evenings that you had to fill with something—whether it was reading, sewing, writing those long letters on those short forces airmail sheets or talking to a friend.

Life for the military family is much like a roller coaster. We experience more highs and lows than most families—having to deal with extended separations, moving every couple of years, buying and selling houses, carting children and pets from place to place, watching our furniture deteriorate more with each move, experiencing job discrimination because your resume reads like a travelogue and you can't guarantee an employer that you will be in one spot for more than two years, helping the kids adjust to their new environment, saying goodbye to family and friends. Believe me, it doesn't get easier, but you do become reasonably skilled in yet another vocation—that of moving large quantities great distances!

Life is a series of challenges. We can either back off, retreat into a shell and blame our husband and the military for our woes . . . or get on with the job at hand and be prepared to deal with the next challenge—and you can be sure that there will be many more ahead—but then, isn't that what life is all about?

I think it is only fair, now, to speak about the positive aspects of being a military wife. I am proud of my husband, who is my biggest supporter in whatever I choose to do, and I am proud to be a military wife. I have had the opportunity to live abroad, travel, make friends throughout the world and to experience wonderful places and things that I might never have had the chance to do, and who knows what the next few years will hold in store for us.

Throughout my life as a military wife, the one constant has been the friendships I have made and am continuing to make. It has been the support, the caring, the understanding, the sharing—by both my military and civilian friends, that has helped me cope, grow as an individual and develop as a person who can contribute to society in a variety of ways, whether in a volunteer or salaried position.

I remember the day I moved into our house in Victoria in

1982. The moving truck had no sooner arrived when the lady across the street appeared with a basket of freshly baked muffins, complete with butter and jam—enough not only for my family but the moving men as well. That day I made a new and dear friend. The friends we make as young wives and mothers often remain lifetime friends.

The message I want to leave you with today is simple— life is short—don't waste even one precious moment of it. You have an opportunity to learn, participate, share. Be proud of who you are and what you are. Seize each and every opportunity. Don't hesitate to reach out, extend a hand—you have nothing to lose and everything to gain. I would like to leave you with a quotation that was given to me by a friend and I have it posted on my fridge as a reminder whenever I feel low and out of sorts—"None so little enjoy life, and are such burdens to themselves, as those who have nothing to do. The active only know the true relish of life."

Chapter 2

Marrying a Military Man– Are You Crazy?

The following article, written by Mrs. Myrann Nickles, appeared in *Sentinel Magazine* in 1978. It is just as true today as the day it was written. This article gives you some insight into just what military wives are letting themselves in for, and why a sense of humour needs to be standard issue. The cartoons were created by Dave Doran.

Condensed from Crash Course in Survival–A Wife's Primer on Living with the Canadian Forces!
by Myrann Nickles

So, you're going to marry a serviceman, are you? Take a friendly tip from a veteran. You're entering a world for which your civilian experiences will not have prepared you. Stand by for a classic case of culture shock.

29

Your transition into the military world will be much easier if you find out as much as you can about that world before you tie the knot. Remember that you will not merely be saying "I do" to the man you marry, but also to all of DND. So, at his weakest moment (usually when he's returned from a lengthy exercise) glean as much as you can about your future, and listen intently to the stories of his "life of adventure."

Then having listened to his tales, take care to sort fact from fiction. The ratio will be about one to ten. Above all, be prepared—for anything. On your wedding day, if it is to be a military wedding, be sure to sport an extra pair of eyes, preferably in the back of your head. Those dignified members of your wedding party are regular Jekels and Hydes, with all manner of fiendish pranks up their sleeves. (Fortunately integration has, for the most part, removed spurs, sabres, swagger sticks and the havoc they can play.)

If you are already finding your sense of humour wearing thin, you'd better repack your bags and go your separate ways. This life doesn't change with age, it just ripens—like any good rotten cheese.

Your debut at his regiment, or whatever working establishment, is a big day for you. To help make the memories pleasant ones, do learn a few basics first—like recognizing rank insignia and hat badges. Then you will at least be able to tell the difference between the CO and the Padre. It is also imperative that your alphabet be at your fingertips in order to understand the 'code' that permeates even the most basic military conversation.

Code conversation (abbreviated forms such as NDHQ) is used partly to speed up boring conversation, and partly because some of the long forms are such impossible mouthfuls that they don't make any sense even to their originators. However, press him for complete explanations so you at least understand the jargon, even if almost no one else does. It may one day stand you in good stead when it's imperative to talk your way out of an otherwise hopeless situation.

For example, you have been pulled over by an MP for running yellow lights. You glare intimidatingly and quickly call upon any nonsense that pops into your head—NDHQ has requested that the 2IC, in absence of the OC, call you into G-311, CFB wherever-it-is STAT to retrieve your husband from an O Group where he's being held for several hours by a hostile CO, Adjt, and various OCs of sqns. No need to explain why—he should be confused enough by now to have forgotten why he stopped you in the first place.

Even that hallowed den of iniquity, the Mess Bar, is no longer sacrosanct. Gone are the days when a woman was tarred and feathered for crossing the threshold and her husband tarred and feathered too, simply for being associated with such

an uncouth, uneducated boor. Today, the skunk has been desensitized—he still has his teeth and claws, and snarls with male indignity when he sees a woman at the bar, but the "odour of sanctity" is gone.

Whether your boy in green belongs to the land, sea or air element, he will be away from home periodically. These field trips are called "exercises," which they sometimes are but on other occasions "lark" would be a more appropriate term. There is no sense in berating him for dashing madly out the door, goggles, pistol, ear-plugs, knife, flashlight and latest issue of *Playboy* flapping about his person, and foolish grin from ear to ear. After all, he has to get away from you, the screaming kids, yapping dogs and other household tedium sometimes. You are now tuned out—i.e., he does not hear you, ear-plugs in or out, so save your breath. At this moment, all he has dancing in his head are APCs, radios, etc. It's disheartening, after struggling to maintain an attractive figure, to learn you are second fiddle to a deuce-and-a-half!

Fortunately, the novelty of this torrid affair wears off in

double quick time. After a couple weeks on RP4s (hard rations), trudging around in inclement weather, sleeping on air mattresses in smelly tents, unable to enjoy the conveniences of hot water and flush toilets, he comes to his senses. You and everything about home are newly appreciated, like new toys again—even the toilet (especially in winter, when every time he patronizes the field facilities, he's taking a chance on posterior (or worse, anterior) frostbite). A word of timely advice: as soon as you spot him on the horizon, scramble to fill the bathtub with water—hot, hot, hot; have the washing machine filled and on red alert, the children locked in a well-ventilated room, and greet him at the door, a smile on your face but Florient in hand. Lack of hot water on exercise, again particularly in winter, is no guff, so what walks in the door closely resembles one giant-size sweaty foot that's been in the same sock for weeks.

To be more cheerful, though, you can look upon these absences as your golden opportunity to accomplish things you can't do when he's home, like taking his closet by storm and pitching out all those ghastly ten-year-out-of-date rags he's been hoarding like a dog does its bones.

Of course, no article such as this would be complete without a discussion of that famous institution of childhood games for grown men, Happy Hour! This is a regular Friday night ritual at messes everywhere (that's right, there's no escape). You are well advised not to prepare dinner until you see your husband in your house in flesh and blood (their games occasionally get a little carried away) and ascertain whether or not he's in any condition to eat. Of course, if the clock ticks past 8 p.m., you may as well quiet your own rumblings and trust that he's had his dinner at the Mess.

Regarded as a perfectly normal occurrence is the tradition of one husband groping his way home, accompanied by half a dozen sidekicks, serving up a much-unneeded drink, and spiriting you away (that's not funny; the fumes are surely 90 proof!) to the next home. They continue thus on the round, collecting wives as they go, and stage an impromptu party at the last house—unannounced of course, much the worse for wear, and often having lost the host somewhere along the way!

This sort of nonsense doesn't begin, usually, the moment you are married. You see, they don't know you yet, and have a healthy respect for your possible explosive reaction. So they pussyfoot around for awhile, turning on the sober, responsible routine, until you relax your vigil.

And we can't forget to mention those great houses they let us rent, the married quarter (MQ or PMQ). Oh, the joys of having one's very first house! But beware the pitfalls, of which there are many. It often happens that PMQ repairs have gone undone, and just try to have them done after you've said "I do" to that house. Even repair orders in writing are no insurance.

It was stated in black and white, with a flourish of red asterisks, when I (I, because my husband was in Cyprus) accepted our first PMQ, that two cracked basement steps were to be replaced immediately, likewise the old metal floor grates on which too many people had ripped open their feet. Someone came twice a year to check for bodies at the bottom of the stairs. When we were marched out 2 1/2 years later, the PMQ was just the same, except the paint in one bedroom, wearing through the yellow to the blue when I moved in, was wearing through the blue to the pink when we moved out.

When, on occasion, someone turns up to fix (or at least tinker with) something, you can expect three people to clomp through the house—one to do the work and two to watch him do it. I'm inclined to think that if each of those three went to do something in three separate homes, a lot more repairs would get done. But who am I to question the wondrous, if confused, workings of CE (Construction Engineering Section)?

The notorious heating system is another fine feature. I often wondered why the kids had perpetual colds during the winter, until I sat on the floor with them one night to watch TV. The gale whistling through the room at floor level turned us blue halfway through Hawaii 5-0. Of course, the thermostat, strategically placed in the warmest corner of the house,  always registers 125° C, although your feet only have the comfort of 15° C temperatures. The ancient fire-breathing dragon in the basement struggles away all winter sucking in any dust floating around the floors, then diligently recycles it all through the pipes, belching clouds of it back into each room.

Every couple of years you get to escape the vagaries of one PMQ for those of another. Depending on your sense of adventure and your outlook about frequent moves, postings can be anything from a nightmare to an intriguing part of your husband's career. We usually settle for a cross between a soap opera and a three-ring circus.

Contrary to much voiced, but frequently inexperienced civvy opinion, children adjust well to the moving routine if their parents' outlook is a good one. "Daddy, those movers snuck my bed onto the truck without boxing it!" (Had to open your big mouth, didn't you kid?) "Mommy, how come we're going to Gagetown and everybody else is going to Germany?" (Yeah, how come?) "Grandma and Grandpa sure must be old. It takes them three weeks just to pack for holidays and we can move our whole house in three days." (ZZzzzzz)

As Forces wives, we probably run the gamut of every emotion known to man, one contradicting the next. Only two things remain stable—the challenge and the lack of boredom. I, for one, wouldn't change it for the world.

And now ladies, if you are still inclined to marry the love of your life and serve as his 'military wife,' read on . . .

The Military Wife

Who said that "Variety is the Spice of Life"?
No doubt 'twas first said by a Military Wife
For the poor girl knows not where she's at;
Her home is wherever HE parks his hat.
She moves each two years into new sets of quarters,
During which time she births sons and daughters.
She packs up to move—Cold Lake's their station
Then orders are changed—they have a new destination.
She may live in a hut with no room for expansion
Or maybe a tent or perhaps it's a mansion.
Then she uncrates the furniture in snow or in rain,
And lays the linoleum between each aching pain.
She wrangles saw horses and builds all the beds,
Makes curtains of hessian she last used for spreads.
And during each move—now isn't it strange?
The brats catch diphtheria, measles or mange!

She no more gets settled when she must dress up pretty,
Go to a party; be charming and witty.
She must know contract rules, mah jong and chess
And whether a straight or a flush is the best.
On every subject she must know how to discourse,
She must swim, ski and golf and ride any troop horse.
She must know traditions of his famous Squadron
And she fast learns the way in which the War was won.
She must drink all concoctions; gin, whiskey and beer
but in moderation or she'll wreck HIS career.

He insists on economy, questions every check stub,
Yet her house must be run like a hotel or club.
For she entertains at all hours, both early and late,
For any number of guests either eighty or eight.
The first of each month there is plenty of cash,
So she serves turkey and ham—but the last week it's hash.

She juggles the budget for a tropical worsted
Though the seams on her own best outfit have bursted
Then she just gets the uniform payments arranged
When the shirt is no good—regulations have changed.
One year she has servants and lives like a lady
The next year she does housework and has a new baby.
That there'll be a bank balance she has no assurance
It all goes for liquor or some damned insurance!

And at an age to retire, HE is hale and hearty,
Fit as a fiddle, the life of the party.
While she's old and haggard, cranky and nervous
Really a wreck after HIS term of service.
But even at that, when all's said and done
She goes on believing that Military Life is Fun!
She has loved every minute—and the reason why
She would have been bored with the average guy.

Then he gets for HIS service the CD
But in actual fact it should have been she!!

Author Unknown

Research as to the identity of the author of the above poem led me from National Defence Headquarters in Ottawa to Shearwater, Nova Scotia to Kingston, Ontario, and I learned that this poem was dedicated to all the wives of 434 Squadron members (Cold Lake, Alberta), past and present, on the occasion of 434 Colour Presentation in the 1980s. Originally an Army poem, some Airforce wives revised it to suit the Air element.

✳   ✳   ✳

What is a serviceman's wife? The following article, which appeared in the *The Base Post*, Petawawa, a few years ago (gleaned from a 20-year-old military newspaper), sums it up:

Serviceman's Wife—A Very Special Person

A serviceman's wife is mostly girl. But there are times such as when her husband is away and she is mowing the lawn or fixing a flat tire of a youngster's bike, that she begins to suspect she is also a boy.

She usually comes in three sizes: petite, plump and pregnant. During the early years of her marriage, it is often hard to determine which size is her normal one.

She has babies all over the world and measures time in terms of places as other women do in years. "It was at Whitehorse that we all had the mumps . . . in Germany Dan was promoted . . ."

At least one of her babies was born or a move accomplished while she was alone. This causes her to suspect a secret pact between her husband and the army providing for a man to be overseas or on temporary duty at times such as these.

A serviceman's wife is international. She may be a prairie farm girl, a French mademoiselle, an Indian princess or a Maritime nurse. When discussing service problems they all speak the same language.

She can be a great actress. To heartbroken children at posting time, she gives an Academy Performance! "Wainwright is going to be such fun, I heard they have Indian Reservations . . . and gophers . . . and more gophers." But her heart is breaking with theirs. She wonders if this service life is worth the sacrifices.

An ideal serviceman's wife has the patience of an angel, the flexibility of putty, the wisdom of a scholar and the stamina of a horse.

If she dislikes money, it helps. She is sentimental, carrying memories with her in an old barrack box. She often cries at parades without knowing why. She is a dreamer when she vows: "We'll never move again." An optimist: "Oh well, as long as we're together."

One might say she is a bigamist sharing her husband with a demanding entity called 'duty.' When duty calls she becomes No. 2 wife. Until she accepts that fact, her life can be miserable.

She is above all, a woman who married a soldier who offered her the permanency of a gypsy, the miseries of loneliness, the frustration of conformity and the security of love.

Sitting among her packing boxes with squabbling children nearby, she is sometimes willing to chuck it all . . . until she hears the firm steps and cheerful voice of that lug who gave her all this.

Then she is happy to be . . . his Serviceman's Wife.

Author Unknown

❋   ❋   ❋

Marrying into the Military

During a military family workshop conducted by John Hanson, the Quality of Life Co-ordinator at the Family Resource Centre in Petawawa, the military wives in attendance had a brainstorming session where they all contributed their ideas and suggestions on "marrying into the military."

After the unanimous "Don't," which produced tons of laughter, some excellent suggestions were voiced, the best of which are repeated here:

- Keep your identity.
- Communication and trust—on both sides.
- Avoid resentment.
- Don't compete with each other.
- Respect each other's individuality.
- Learn to be accepting.
- Develop new skills.
- It doesn't come easily—work at it.

- What you give now comes back to you later.
- Have a strong sense of humour.
- Learn how to do everything yourself.
- Don't get pregnant too soon.
- Enjoy the life as much as you can.
- Turn the negatives into positives.
- Don't feel guilty about your feelings.
- Never suffer in silence—you are not a martyr.
- Have a military marriage preparation course.
- Don't say things when you're angry.
- Don't allow your family to be treated as soldiers.
- Be adventurous—expand your horizons.
- It's OK to feel you're alone—but you're not.
- Learn how to do all the banking.

Advice

The women I contacted also had useful advice for new wives. It was interesting to note how often the response was the same: "Be yourself"; "Be patient, become independent, and make time for yourself" top the list. Much of this advice applies to any wife regardless of her husband's occupation. We military wives have the advantage of a 'network.' So many wives whose husbands are not in the forces do not experience that feeling of "belonging," nor do they have the opportunity to gather as a group and learn from each other, which is often therapeutic in itself.

This life is a choice you make. I have a friend whose husband is a consultant all over the world and she has no network.

Stand fast, mate. You're in for a rough ride. If you can hang onto the railing throughout the storm which lasts about 10 years, you've got it made!

Expect the worst—hope for the best.

Get involved in your community. Great way to make new friends and it helps you to settle a lot quicker.

Make everyday life as rich as possible and value the family life. Create self-esteem.

Make the most of the lifestyle—it has some good things to offer—focus on those.

Make sure your husband or future husband doesn't drink (or knows how to drink). Those TGIF come every week, 52 times a year!

Go into your military life with an open mind, a giving heart, a smile and a bottle of aspirin!

Don't stay in the house all day.

Make one really good friend that you can talk to. Have other friends but only one really close. Don't sit around the neighbor's house all day drinking coffee. She has a life too!

Be prepared to make an identity for yourself apart from military life.

Don't believe anything unless it is in "black and white."

Be there for your children—one parent away is enough!

Be patient—give your marriage a chance. It's not all that bad—you have to be strong enough for the both of you—for your marriage and your children.

Be flexible.

Always go to the new posting with an open mind and not "I'm not going to like it . . . "

Be patient. He will grow up. He will realize that you will always be there even when all his friends are busy, even when the army has really upset him. Learn what his job is, what the army does. Listen to what he talks about, become involved—it helps in communication. It all affects your life too so you might as well learn it.

The military is your career as well as your husband's. Discuss with your husband what you expect from each other because it's hard to change your expectations later on.

After the courtship and acceptance of the man and the lifestyle (they come as a package deal . . .) comes the stepping into the military world. For many, that is when realization really sets in, that's when the honeymoon is over . . .

Chapter 3

The Honeymoon's Over

Once you have settled into life as a military wife, it helps to remember that men react with their brain but women react with their emotions. Also, the military seems to produce these guys who believe it's not 'macho' to show personal emotions. They have to be tough, strong and fearless. The sooner you understand the two sides to your mate (the military side and the side he shows you), the easier your life will be.

Marriage to a Gunner

Romance is sweet, a gentle time
You're both in love, the wedding set
You're on your way to PMQs
You are about to pay your dues
You're married to a Gunner.

The life is pleasant on the Base,
You're learning at an easy pace,
The Artillery jargon, schemes, parades,
Spit and polish to make the Grade.
You find a job, you're settled fine
The house all fixed, the flowers up

It's all too good to last of course
The posting wire will make it clear
You have to follow HIS *career*
You're married to a Gunner!

The years go by, he's on his way
He loves his job, what can you say,
Some days you'd like to run away
That's marriage to a Gunner!

But when he's home, how sweet it is
The quiet evenings, Sunday walks
Between the phone calls, family talks
You plan a dinner to impress
But where is he? Still at the Mess!
You're married to a Gunner!

Don't cry the blues, you've made your bed
You follow your heart instead of your head,
When you could have been bored to death instead
Of married to a Gunner!

A gift to Mia Beno from her friend Edna Pollack

Disillusionment

When we got married I didn't know a thing about military life
and my husband didn't really explain anything to me. He was
already in the military when we met and I can remember think-
ing 'good government job.' Great, we will be living in a real
luxurious lifestyle. I had thought military people made tons of
money! We have been married for four years and I am still
trying to find the money!

It is hard when my husband is away. He was away for two
months this time and I had tons of butterflies in my stomach.
When he was due home it was just like starting our relationship
all over. I get mad at him for going away. Sometimes I hate him
for it. The days just before he goes away I am not happy at all. I
get upset with myself for feeling this way but I just can't help it.

In the first year we were married, he was away on exercise in the middle of winter. I was feeling very lonely and depressed so I called the unit and asked if they could get a message to my husband to call me, this was 2 a.m. Well, when he got the message he was worried that something serious was wrong and he called right away. I just wanted to tell him I was lonesome. I'll never forget his reaction. He said, "Are you crazy? Do you know what time it is? I am standing here freezing talking into a phone hooked up to a tree. Get a grip on yourself!"

✳   ✳   ✳

In the first year we were married my husband was away about six months off and on. We were married in Germany in 1966 and lived on the economy (civilian housing). All my husband said to me beforehand was that the housing over there was not quite up to Canadian standards. What he didn't tell me was that our apartment was upstairs in a 100+-year-old building. The back half that originally housed the animals had been boarded up on the side facing the street and the whole building had been condemned. You looked out our kitchen window into a small overgrown inner courtyard and there was still straw sticking out of the window areas of the back half of the building—which had neither glass nor frames. The kitchen floor was so uneven that when I washed it the water all ran to one side. There was mildew on all the walls and the only sink was in the kitchen. We shared an unheated bathroom with an old German couple, and it was located outside our apartment in a room off the main hallway. It consisted of tub and toilet and water tank only. If you wanted to take a bath you built a fire at the bottom of the water tank with paper and sticks and kept it going with coal briquettes which we bought by the bagfull. Once the water was hot you had your bath regardless of whether company dropped in because if you didn't, the water would cool off and you would have to start the procedure all over again.

The next year we moved to the downstairs apartment. It had more mildew, but did have its own bathroom inside the apartment. The large living-room window looked out onto the back yard of the house next door which was on a slightly higher level. Our view was the chicken coop and a yard full of chickens. Every once in a while you'd see a rat run up the ramp into the hen house . . . We had no phone, no TV and no car—but *we were happy*. We knew we didn't have to live like that forever and we took advantage of seeing as much of Europe as we could.

International Births

A problem that frequently surfaced in my talks with the wives was dealing with pregnancies and births while their husbands were away. Most of these stories will be found in Chapter 10, since many of these experiences occurred when husbands were on UN taskings.

While the military tries to be as accommodating as possible, there are times when our husbands just aren't able to be with us, regardless of how much they would like to be. I was very fortunate in having my husband at home for the birth of both of our sons, but I'd like to share with you here the difference I found having one child in Germany and the other in Canada.

I became ill while my husband was away on exercise. After diagnosing myself as having the flu and a bladder infection, I knew after the fourth day of 24-hour sickness that this 'bug' was like no other I had ever experienced. My husband arrived home on the fifth day and, after taking one look at me (I'd lost 8 lbs.), he whisked me off in a taxi (we had no car) to the military medical clinic. No doctor was present as it was on the weekend, so I was taken in an ambulance (I insisted on riding in the front) four kilometres away where the doctor was waiting on base to see me. My suspicions were confirmed—this 'flu' was to last for nine months but I would be richly rewarded when it was over. I was indeed pregnant! Things went along normally until my eighth month, when the doctor said he was admitting me to the hospital because of a few complications. We had no phone and my husband was confined to barracks four kilometres away on his pre-junior course. I was alone, scared and really didn't know what to do or how to contact my husband. The neighbour downstairs drove into camp and told my husband what was happening and that I would have to go to the hospital the next day. He slipped out of barracks and came to see me, knowing he was AWOL and would be in trouble if he was caught. But all he could do was spend a few minutes with me to find out how I was and exactly what was going on. I cried myself to sleep that night and really wondered what I had let myself in for, being thousands of miles from family and friends and having a husband who was away just as much as he was home.

The next day I took a taxi to the military medical clinic and waited for the military bus to take me to the British Military Hospital, which was used by the Canadians. It was a half-hour drive away. There I was, big as a barrel, trying to lift my suitcase onto the bus—there was no one to help me; the bus driver just sat and watched me struggling. I didn't know what lay ahead. I have never felt so alone or scared in my life!

However, I survived the crisis and our son Chris was born right on schedule with no complications.

Having visited friends who had children in Canadian hospitals, I was not prepared for the very different treatment at the British hospital, which was very regimented. We had to walk to the nursery to feed our babies. After the third day we were responsible for bathing our children every morning. Sometimes you'd walk to the nursery three or four times before a space would be available.

There was only one washroom on each floor—at the opposite end of the hall from my room (there were four beds to a room). So we certainly did our share of walking! Daily exercises were compulsory and done as a group. Meals were served in the lounge—if you didn't show up, you didn't eat. The meal was very greasy and a daily serving of stewed prunes wasn't any more appetizing. After about 5-7 days I was released.

Our second son Trevor was born in Oromocto, New Brunswick, and I thought I'd died and gone to heaven! Despite his extremely fast arrival on the gurney wheeling me into the delivery room, I felt completely 'spoiled' in comparison to my earlier experience. I was alone in the room and really enjoyed my time with my son, and I did get more rest. These long hospital stays for childbirth seem to be a thing of the past; but no matter how long your stay, my friends, be thankful when you have your children in Canada!

When we were first married I was really apprehensive about being alone in the house. My husband went away for 12 weeks and I was pregnant at the time. But after I'd survived that long spell alone, I decided that it was quite an accomplishment for me and I was proud of myself.

Prejudice

If civilians were more open-minded about us as individuals, I think our life would be much more simple. I hate being told my husband must be alcoholic, unfaithful and generally 'Pongo' just because he wears a uniform. And it's always by people who have never even met him!

As with any group, military men are sometimes judged by the negative actions of a few. In my own life, growing up in the navy port of Halifax, nice girls just didn't date sailors. It wasn't something that was particularly discussed at home; it was just something that *was*. Added to the local population of sailors, in the summer there were always American ships in port and it was not an accepted thing to date any sailors, especially Americans. We heard very early that "Sailors have a girl in every port!"

When I was about 19 I met an American who was serving on a submarine which was in port for a few days. By then I was old enough to want to make my own decisions and form my own opinions and not be guided by other people's prejudices. So we dated. He was a very nice young man, a long way from home.

But what was upsetting to me one evening, as we walked to a nearby restaurant for supper, were the unkind comments from some local fellows walking by. "What's the matter, aren't we good enough for you?" was one of several comments. We ignored the men as well as their comments, but it genuinely bothered both of us. It was my first experience with prejudice, and I didn't like it. How could they make assumptions when they didn't know either of us?

A few years later my brother had joined the Navy and my sister had married a Navy man. It disturbed me that there were people out there thinking that my brother and brother-in-law were 'second-class citizens,' people to avoid simply because they were wearing uniforms. Couldn't they see that these two men were making a contribution to society and their families? Couldn't they see the only thing different about them as compared with their own sons and brothers was that they had a job that required them to be away from home and they were easily identified because they all wore the same clothing?

Over the years, working on military bases, I have had the opportunity to speak with many young servicemen. These men on the whole are better adjusted, more independent and more responsible than a lot of the local men. There is good and bad wherever you go, but the wearing of a uniform should not automatically label these men 'second class.' Unfortunately, that prejudice is still alive today. Is it the fear of the unknown? Don't people realize that each of these young men is somebody's son, brother, uncle? Does being in the military really make them *that* different?

For some women meeting a guy, falling in love, getting married and living happily ever after is not as easy as it appears. Local girls living close to a military base often have a problem with prejudice in their family towards military men. Below is one young woman's story of being a 'local girl,' dealing with prejudice, and marrying the army man who was the love of her life.

I dated the son of a local friend of my father's for four years, and that was OK with Dad, but he had problems dealing with it when I started to date an Army guy. He was really into "What will the neighbors think?" He made me feel bad, as if I was just out looking for Army guys. He made me feel really cheap. When I started dating my husband, Dad said he'd be glad when all this 'army business' was over. But when our relationship became serious, Dad said he didn't like the Army because I would have to move away. Still, once he got to know my husband he really liked him and now my husband can drop over to my parents' house without me and feel quite at home. My Mom's been OK through all this because her father was in the military.

When my husband and I talked about getting married, he said he wouldn't marry me while he was in the military because it would take me away from my family and friends. I have lived in this house my whole life and my friends are all friends that I have had since I started school. But today the military is a steady job and I want to accompany my husband; I'm excited about travelling to new places. I think it will be a real adventure, although it will be hard to leave everyone I've known all my life.

I was the first one in my group of friends to date a military man. Now that they've met him and socialized with us and see that he really is a very nice guy, they are thinking that maybe it's OK to date an Army man and that maybe they can find a nice guy too! Now my sister is engaged to a really nice guy from the military.

The Fine Line

One of the most difficult things in this lifestyle, besides learning that you don't always come first in your husband's life, is the need to compromise. There has to be compromise in every marriage, but in the military marriage it is way up there in importance right next to trust and communication. Finding that centre line where you each meet halfway can be very difficult.

The serviceman has been away 'forever' and just looks forward to coming home and staying there—enjoying his home life after the rigours of living in a tent, eating hard rations or living in quarters while away on course. But on the other hand, during this same period of time his wife has been somewhat tied to the house, kids and all the responsibilities. So when her partner comes home, she is looking forward to dressing up, going out with her husband, talking to adults for a change and leaving kids, house and responsibilities behind. Finding that centre line which meets both needs can be a very difficult task—something you have to continually work at. He must realize that her social contacts have more or less circled around the kids and their needs while he was away, and she must realize that he needs some time to unwind, catch up on his sleep and adjust to a regular routine again.

I was born in England and we were married there, so when we came to Canada I really was a 'stranger in a strange land.' I found it lonely, of course, but when you are that young you can put up with a lot more. I'm not sure the young ones of today would be so patient.

I find that we wives become very regimented in our routine — out of necessity. Especially when our husbands are away. You just have so much to do to manage everything; I find at times I really am impatient. If I ask my husband to do something for me, I want it done now, not in 5-10 minutes' time. It's really not that I am always that demanding, but I just want it done so I can get it off my mind and move on to something else. If he doesn't respond right away, then I get mad and go do it myself . . .

I asked the wives if they ever shine their husbands' boots. Inevitably this question seemed to give the women their 'chuckle of the day.' Responses ranged from "You're not serious!"; "Are you crazy? I'm not!"; "Not on your life!"; "Yeah, right! As if I have nothing else to do!" ; "Sure, I shine them faithfully every day. Ha, ha."

However, there was one young woman who admitted that she really did do her husband's boots. When I asked her why, she said, "Because he'd never be ready on time if I didn't . . ."

Peer Pressure

Several young wives commented on peer pressure and how it was affecting their marriage. It seems that peer pressure does not end when school is out, and some wives find this difficult to deal with. Their husbands want to be 'accepted,' and so sometimes follow a course of action that is not going to be accepted by their wives. Conflicts arise and, while this is all a part of maturing and growing as an individual, it can take a little longer and be a little more intense in the military atmosphere than elsewhere.

Walk a Mile

Having to deal with their husbands' long absences, many wives become frustrated with family and civilian friends who moan and groan about their husbands going away for a day or two, or a friend absolutely refusing to stay alone in the house when her husband was away. They have little or no patience for these women who feel so hard done by. "Walk a mile in *my* shoes . . ."

When I go home for visits I get really upset at my friends and family and their complaining about small things. Sure, being separated from their husbands for a few days is a big deal to them, but they do not understand how much we have to deal with things like this—sometimes thousands of miles away from family. We have to stick it out and make the best of it.

My husband was on a UN tour and we lived close to my family. I really thought my sisters would understand how hard it was for me to be alone so much; I thought they would visit me more. But I guess they were busy with their own lives. You have to be a part of this life to understand the loneliness . . .

Mrs. General

One questionnaire asked the wives for their husband's rank (no names were required), and this was followed by a blank space to fill in the wife's rank. This was originally inserted to find out how many wives responding to the survey were also in the military. However, once again the women suprised me. Their answers to this question showed that they definitely want to be recognized as individuals rather than extensions of their husbands.

They almost always 'ranked' themselves at least one rank higher than their husbands. A few showed an even greater sense of humour by ranking themselves way at the top of the scale with many 'generals' surfacing. Of course this was usually followed with a 'just joking . . .' One woman *really* 'topped' the scale, filling in her husband's rank as 'Captain' and hers as "One above my husband's and two below God!"

Remember When

Most people my age have lots of stories we could tell about our lives, but I think there is one thing that many of us forget. And this applies to our husbands as well when dealing with their work relationships. We forget how traumatic are some of the difficulties young couples have had to face alone. We can look back now, and chuckle at all we had to deal with way back then, but at the time there was nothing funny in dealing with the situation. We just plain forget how devastating it can be for the young to handle all that is sometimes thrown at them. The attitude of some older military members and their wives is "What's wrong with them, we had to deal with much more and we survived!" Let's try to remember what it was really like when we were young.

Anxiety

Many wives over the years have been upset over the military's general reaction to women who have suffered anxiety attacks. Some do take it far too lightly—comparing it with a headache, and labelling women who suffer from it as 'just another neurotic military wife,' or 'someone who just can't get her act together . . .' If you have never experienced an anxiety attack, you can't possibly know how terrifying it can be; I speak from experience. Once you have suffered through one, you then are a little better prepared, but that doesn't lessen the anxiety in trying to deal with a second one. Finding the reason for the attack can take time, and until you know what is causing it, you are not able to prevent it from happening again. Unfortunately, in trying to adjust to our lifestyle, many wives experience this problem. According to medical personnel, these anxiety attacks are very common among military wives and usually occur when the men are on UN taskings or training for one. What some in the military seem to forget is that a lot of wives, young ones in particular, are dealing with a whole myriad of emotions all at the same time—from loneliness, frustration, indecision and apprehension, to trying to cope all alone with no family support handy. They deserve more understanding from the military . . .

Medical Help

Finding a good doctor and babysitter are two of the most necessary and sometimes most difficult things to accomplish when moving to a new area. There are far too many times when doctors treat a military wife as if her illness is 'all in her head' and label her as 'just another lonesome military wife looking for a little attention . . .' If you find you are getting that kind of response from your doctor and are not being treated as an individual, then change doctors. He/ she is not going to be objective in dealing with your problems if he/she comes across with that kind of an attitude. We are all individuals who share a common lifestyle, but we *must* be treated as individuals by all professionals.

Advantages

While negative comments might overshadow some positive sections of this book, I feel it necessary to really 'tell it like it is'—negative and positive. However, there are many, many advantages to the lifestyle and one of the most significant ones is personal growth. Many of the things you will have to deal with and accomplish will be beyond anything you could have dreamed about when you said "I do!" Some of your civilian friends will comment, "I don't know how you do it, I couldn't." The response to that remark is very simple—you do it because you have to. And with each decision made alone, each crisis handled by yourself, you are learning and growing and becoming stronger. You *can* do it— no matter what it is. If someone had told me that someday I would be writing a book, I would probably have laughed and said, "Yes, and I'm really Elizabeth Taylor's twin!"

Many of the women I talked with can't believe their good fortune in being able to live the life they have. Unanimously, the wives list travelling and experiencing different cultures at the top of the advantage list, but here are other comments:

> *There are advantages to this lifestyle for the whole family. Wherever we were posted there have always been gym facilities, hockey rink, curling rink and a golf course handy, just to name a few. The military gets special rates at most civilian recreational facilities, and our family has been able to participate in all the sports activities we wanted. But it's certain that if we were civilians these facilities would not all be so handy, or affordable either!*

> *Here in Petawawa everyone is so fortunate with all the clubs on base—ceramics, pottery, oil painting, badminton, computer, etc. It's so easy to take them all for granted until you get post-*

ed to another base and find little in comparison. Then you
wish you had taken advantage of some of the things that
appealed to you on the last base instead of putting it off.

For Better or for Worse

To close this chapter, here are a few words for all you husbands who
have shown enough interest in your wife and military wives in general to
read this book. For those
wives whose husbands have
not had a chance to read this
book yet, why not ask him to
read these next few lines:

"Marriage is an institu-
tion." "Marriage is like an old
shoe—after a while it becomes
quite comfortable and you
don't want to do without it!"
We have all heard these or similar phrases at one time or
another. Many of us have also
come across articles in
women's magazines on how to
keep the 'spark' alive in your
marriage. I am sure there are
as many varied opinions on the
worth of these articles as there
are women reading them!

As newlyweds, you gaze into each other's eyes and vow never to be
apart. It always works in the romance novels, but somehow falls a little
short when the husband is a military man!

So, like most military wives, you try to make the most of the time
you do have together, and probably because of the long separations
throughout the year separate vacations are far from your thoughts.
However, as the years pass by and hubby has 'done his time' in Alert,
Cyprus, Golan or wherever, you begin to think that maybe living away
from wifey and kids in a lovely hot (or cold) climate with no responsibilities other than doing his job, shining his boots and deciding what to eat

for supper (which he doesn't have to cook)—maybe, just maybe, there is a little bit of a holiday atmosphere here, besides serving our Country!

While you're up to your knees in snow, shovelling the driveway, it's hard to feel sorry for your guy who is probably working on his tan. While you're trying to get Junior to stop dumping his carrots on his sister's plate, *he* is trying to decide whether he wants a second piece of coconut cream pie. While you're flopping into a chair after giving all the kids their baths, stopping them from fighting, giving each one their last drink of water and organizing the inevitable pee parade, and finally the house is reasonably quiet, you're too exhausted to even think of going to a movie. Besides, with *him* away for umpteen months there are extra expenses, and since you had to get a new battery for the car (it worked fine until *he* left . . .), there isn't any extra money left to treat yourself to a movie and pay a sitter until next payday.

Now, guys, don't you dare say that's what VCRs are for! I'm sure any wife who has survived a long separation can tell you how ugly those same four walls become after a while.

Yes, I know it's not easy on the guys being away—they can't hear wifey's requests: "For the fourth time, when are you going to clean up the basement?" "Don't forget to mow the lawn before you go out with the guys." They can't snuggle in their Lazyboy, wait for wifey to get up and "While you're up, Hon, how about getting me another beer?" Poor things! Seriously though, guys, you have the best of both worlds, as any wife will tell you.

So, if you have found that special woman who loves you as you are, and tries to understand why 'duty calls' take priority over her requests, then count your blessings. A military wife is a special breed. When you finally come home and hear her say, "Next time you stay home with the kids and I'll go on exercise," realize that she is serious, and that it's time to take a step back, look at this woman who is there 'for better or for worse' and do your utmost to make sure there is more 'better' and less 'worse'!

Chapter 4

Wives, Mistresses and Significant Others

Military wives are as diversified a group as there ever was. They come from all walks of life and every nationality. Besides having in common their love for a military man, they share another common bond. Each one of them is a mistress . . .

Mistresses

When you are young and newly married, you vow that you are going to make your husband the focal point of your life—he is always going to come first no matter what. And in return, you expect that you will come first in his life. Well, unfortunately, a military wife has to learn to take second place. You are his mistress, sharing whatever time he can squeeze away from his 'wife'—that is, his job. Having your time together is possible only when his 'wife' is not making demands. You may have your plans changed at the last minute because his 'wife' needs him elsewhere.

It's not easy taking second place in your husband's life, but it does happen, and as with any man who has two loves, he is often caught right in the middle, trying to please both at the same time—often an impossible task! His 'wife' comes first—although this is not necessarily of his own choosing.

This can be a hard lesson to learn, but the sooner you accept it and deal with it, the easier it will be on everyone. Besides, don't you feel like his naughty mistress sometimes when he has been away for a long time, and you have the romantic setting in the bedroom waiting for his return—complete with scented candles, soft lights, romantic music and your sexiest black lace teddy? Sure you do!

> *In Germany we had not seen the guys for three months. They were away on exercise. So three friends and I got babysitters, rented an orange Volkswagen and drove the 150 miles to a restricted area where the guys were located. It took us eight hours to get there. We had packed a big picnic basket complete with wine, cheese and red and black nighties. We went looking for our husbands. Finally we managed to get hold of one of the husbands by phone. We said we were coming to where they were and he said, "Don't do that or we will get kicked out of the Army!" We said we were going to a village nearby anyway, so they had better be there, and we told them we would be at a certain square at midnight. Well, we arrived there and the place was deserted; then we spotted the guys— all four of them. They sneaked out of camp and had rented some rooms at a dirty old motel, where we stayed the night. We were walking down the hall the next morning and who do we see but my husband's Sergeant and even the Commanding Officer—they had all snuck their wives down to the motel too! Were we all surprised!*

Performance Evaluation Reports

As anyone involved with the military is aware, annual performance evaluation reports (PERs) are completed for each military and civilian employee. This is a yearly assessment of the individual's work performance by his supervisors. Both a narrative and a scoring system are used.

Since my husband and I have received many PERs over the years, and since the military format and grading is quite different from the civilian format, the outcomes of our assessments have always generated interesting conversation in our house. He claims my PER would not be that high if I worked for him and I retaliate by saying he'd never get to do a PER on my work performance because I would no doubt quit after the first week!

Having cleared the air on that point, it occurred to me what a good idea PERs are and just how much they could be used in other areas of our lives.

Ladies, what about doing a PER on your husband? Settle down, guys, I'm not referring to a sexual performance evaluation report—although that idea does have some merit!

A few likely categories come to mind, and I'm sure most of you wives will agree. On a rating scale of 1-10 with 10 being the highest, you could rate hubby on the following, for starters:

1. He cooks supper without any suggestions or hints from me just to give me a break.

2. He runs my bath water complete with bubble bath, scented candles and a chilled glass of wine within easy reach,

puts my favourite tape on the stereo, then switches on the answering machine and takes the kids to McDonald's.

3. He lets me sleep in on the weekends, quietly doing household chores.

4. He consistently hangs up all his clothes.

5. He volunteers to address all the Christmas cards.

6. He not only does the wash, but folds the clothes when they come out of the dryer—and matches *all* the socks.

Items for this list are endless and could be personalized to suit your particular relationship. However, to give the men equal time, may I suggest some likely points?

1. She spit-shines my combat boots.

2. She irons my uniform with *no* double creases.

3. She shovels the driveway so I can watch my hockey game.

4. Even though she often ends up being right, she never says "I told you so!"

5. She doesn't mind being called Peg Bundy!

6. She picks all the bones out of my fish and peels my cooked potatoes before serving me supper.

7. She laughs at all my jokes.

Now you get the idea, friends. But whether any of you decide to implement this interesting format in your daily life or not, the bottom line here is that *none* of us likes to be taken for granted.

Infidelity

Although many wives survive the military lifestyle, some don't. The following interview was with one who did not, and four hours after it started, this interview left both her and me emotionally drained. I often thought how different her story might have turned out today, because wives are less isolated and there are more support avenues out there. What this woman's story showed me is how totally and utterly alone some wives can feel even when they are surrounded by others.

We met at a bar where he was moonlighting as a bartender and at first I didn't know he was in the military. He was so utterly handsome and charming that when he asked me out, of course I said yes. I couldn't believe that he wanted to be with me. As we dated, I became so proud of him. He was very active in sports and he was so different from the other guys. Then I became pregnant and when I was about six months along, he left. The scene was just not one he wanted to pursue. Then he was posted away.

I had a son who weighed 2 lbs. and was not expected to live. Unknown to me, my girlfriend telephoned him and told him about his son and said, "How can you do this to her? How can you leave her to face all this alone?" He did come around and our son survived—in fact he is a strong, handsome man in his late 20s today. We started dating again when he could come to the area where I lived, and when our son was three years old we married. But we were just kids playing at being adults. We were so young and we really didn't have time for romance in our marriage, starting off the way we did. We did not have enough experience to realize that *we* were important, not the military.

In retrospect, our beginning was on shakier ground than I realized. He came from a very unhappy family life, and I came from a very large family. My father, who was a military man, died when Mom was 30, so we never had much.

I always had a structured life, so the military lifestyle appealed to me because it was also a structured existence. I really liked the life. I met a real man who had money, a car, who could crush beer cans with his teeth, was always smartly dressed, had neat haircuts and was liked by everyone. It was all so appealing.

A year after we were married I had another son. Then we were posted to Germany for four years before returning to Canada. My husband made the decisions and I followed. I adored him, I loved him more than life itself and I totally devoted myself to him and the boys. I always felt that I had to be everything to him so that he would be happy. It was my job to always comfort him—to be there for him. Everyone thought we had a perfect marriage, including me.

It was always so important for him to be liked by his buddies and for him to spend time with them. I absolutely hated Happy Hours. No matter what, Friday nights belonged to him and his friends, and the boys and I were excluded. He felt he 'earned' Friday nights and I really resented it. On Saturdays he was recovering from Friday night. That's when I got groceries, so he figured if I wasn't home then there was no need for him to be home, and he would go play sports.

Because of his involvement in so many sports, I spent a lot of time alone. Then he had an affair and was going to leave me, but his father, who wasn't well and had come to live with us, talked him out of it. So instead he volunteered to go on a six-month UN tour. There I was holding down a full-time job, as well as managing a business venture we had both started, caring for his father, looking after the boys and making all the decisions alone. My weight went down to 92 lbs.

When he came back he remustered to another trade and we were posted to Kingston. On Canada Day, after we had returned from taking the boys to watch the fireworks, he told me he just didn't want to be married anymore. He just said he could no longer live a lie and that I had placed him so high on a pedestal that he just couldn't live up to that anymore. "You thought I was so perfect, but there were always girls when I was away . . ." He said he just couldn't do that to me any more and that when he looked at his life he didn't like what he saw, so he wanted out. He remained in Kingston and I returned home with the boys and his father, who refused to stay with him—and he remained with me until he died.

The boys were devastated—they adored their father and kept asking when he was coming home. I thought all this must just be a misunderstanding, and I decided that all I needed to do was bake his favourite cookies and go talk to him and then everything would be all right and he would come back to me. Well, when I got to where he was living and realized that he had another woman living with him, I felt like a fool for thinking all I needed to do was just talk this whole thing out with him. It was then that I realized our lives had changed forever and it was time I got on with my life—without him. It was so hard for me to go home and to tell the boys, "No, your father will not be coming back."

He lived the life of a bachelor, but after about 7-8 months he called and wanted to come home. Life was far from what he expected it to be. But I knew in my heart that I just could not forgive him. He went through a really rough time then. He really struggled with all this and right in the middle put in his release from the forces. I really blame the military for not being there for him. He was not in the right emotional state to make that decision, and before he knew it he found himself a civilian again. When we were having problems we didn't want to talk to the Padre, as we felt if we did then it would affect his career. It's ironic that his career ended anyway . . . I really think though that if there had been someone he could have talked to when he was struggling with all that he was, my life and his would have turned out differently. He always knew what he had to do in the army—he was always told what to do each day, but then when you get out of the army it's so different—he really didn't know where he belonged.

I can't tell you of the years of struggling as a single mother, of the boys who resented their father so much for leaving us, of the difficult time they gave any man that I became interested in.

My present husband and I dated for four years and then we married when my oldest son was 18. After all these years I still can't believe how very fortunate I am to have a man who is totally devoted to me, just as I was to my ex-husband. I keep expecting the bubble to burst. He loves the boys as his own and we are both good friends with my ex-husband. How many men could feel confident enough in themselves and their relationship with their wife to do that? He is one in a million and I thank God every day for him. But, you know, there is still a small part of me that holds back—waiting for the roof to cave in again. The scars I carry run very deep.

When this lady agreed to talk with me she had no idea what she could say as a military wife, because that period of her life was so long ago. But during our conversation she remembered things that she hadn't thought about in years. She dealt with many mixed emotions—on the one hand feeling that because her military marriage was not successful to the end, it should be discounted, but on the other hand feeling it definitely could not be discounted because, regardless of the outcome, it was an important part of her life and had produced her two sons, whom she loves very much. To discount it would be as if all of them just didn't exist for those years.

At times during our conversation I felt her emotions rushing close to the surface, but she managed to keep them in check until the interview was finished, when she couldn't hold back the tears any longer. "I feel so different—you know, I think I just validated my life as a military wife! I can say I was a military wife—and it's OK!" Yes, my friend, it is indeed OK—you were a military wife and you were, and are, special . . .

None of us knows what tomorrow will bring or, when tomorrow comes, whether we will be facing something similar to this woman's story. Separation and divorce, as well as health problems, are not restricted to any age group.

With this mobile lifestyle, the struggles many of the military wives face balancing careers and families are tremendous. More often than not, the wives have had to sacrifice their careers. How then do some of these wives face divorce and separation—some after 20-30 years of marriage? By then their husbands are either embarking on second careers or preparing to do so, the kids have grown up and gone from home and the wives are no doubt thousands of miles from their relatives. There she is, middle-aged, with rusty or outdated work skills, all alone facing the nightmare of trying to support herself. All this at a time in her life when she should be reaping the rewards middle age is 'supposed' to bring.

Our friends were all really his military friends. So when we separated I cut myself off from them so they wouldn't have to 'choose.' Sometimes I wish I hadn't . . .

While divorce and separation affect every lifestyle, it is particularly harsh and unfair in the military setting. With today's economy and a shortage of jobs, how is the middle-aged ex-military wife going to fare? Does anyone care?

However, not all stories of infidelity end in separation or divorce, and more than one wife has shared with me the agonies of facing the 'truth' in their marriage and trying to move on from there as a couple. As in any marriage, once the trust has been devastatingly broken, it can be a tremendous job to trust again. Here is a story from the other side of the infidelity coin. We pick up on it after the emotional upheaval had somewhat subsided.

I felt that I had worked very hard at our marriage, our home and our lifestyle and was not about to give up on it without a fight! In the beginning, as we tried to rebuild our relationship, I had no idea if we would ever make it. There were good days and bad days and days when I asked myself 'What in hell am I doing here?' The mistrust crept out at every corner. My health suffered and I really didn't know if I was doing the right thing. Some days that apartment by myself looked so inviting . . .

We adored our children and I thought we had had a good life. This lifestyle had made me independent enough that I had no doubts I could manage OK on my own, but I kept asking myself—did I want to? Did I want to separate forever from this man I had devoted my life to, from our home that took so many years to attain, from the lifestyle we had created? Some days yes and some days no. I think a little of my heart has been permanently closed and I doubt if it will ever re-open. I know that no man will ever be allowed to hurt me that much again and I also know that my husband will have to live with how he has hurt me for the rest of his life.

But no one is perfect and I don't blame him entirely for what happened. The shock of his actions caused me to really re-examine our life together and my own actions and although

I was never unfaithful, I didn't always like what I saw in the mirror. I think now that we have reached a new level in our relationship. There is a new maturity between us, a new understanding. I remember telling our children right in the middle of the emotional upheaval that every marriage is tested at one time or another and that the love my husband and I had for each other would see us through this test—and it has. I have no doubts now that I made the right decision for me.

This woman went on to say that while the military lifestyle might have contributed to the initial breakdown in the marriage, it also contributed to its survival! Being alone, being so far from family, the requirements to be responsible and decisive all help build character. The lifestyle continually tests us as individuals. "I was always so shy and had so little confidence. But my lifestyle has changed that out of necessity. I really don't know if I would have been able to make the decisions I have if I had led a different lifesytle. I think not."

Blended Families

In blended families, a new wife, with or without children of her own, trying to fit into an established family and be accepted by those children can find it very difficult. Problems are magnified when it is a military family, constantly on the move:

It is similar, I think, to being a foster child or a poor relative. When I meet with other service wives, the 'remember when' and 'do you remember so and so' are all part of a shared history that I have no knowledge of. That shared history sets me apart and makes me very uncomfortable. Likewise with the outside community, now; I am a stranger and have no ties there either. However, despite the rejection of some and the curiosity of several, I have made friends in the community.

What I'm trying to say is: The military wives are very cliquish and the outside community is not particularly inviting or welcoming of the people on the base. So, unfortunately, one finds oneself away from family with no welcoming place to socialize.

I feel as if I arrived for the last act of a very good production. It's a terrible and wonderful lifestyle. My only regret is that I didn't arrive in time for the beginning. I would have liked to have been a part of the history, the travel and all that I hear from the other wives.

After several years as an observer, let me say I take my hat off to those of you who have set so much aside and made a home wherever the military sent you. I think you can look back and be very proud of your success.

It's My Life Too

There was one time that was difficult for us. My husband had been away for about two months and the night he was coming home was the last playoff night for my bowling team. I was very excited about his return but felt obligated to the team—we had worked so hard all season and had a good chance of winning the playoffs—but I had to play, as we weren't allowed substitutes. So, since it was only a matter of about two hours that he would be home before me, I told my husband that I would be right home after bowling. I arranged to be the first one up to bowl on my team and all night I thought of him and left the alley like a flash as soon as I was finished. We had won, but I didn't stay around long enough to find out!

But he wasn't home. He had stopped off in town for a few drinks with the boys. This was the first time that I had ever put myself first instead of him and he was really upset that I wasn't going to be there to greet him; if I wasn't home he didn't see the need to rush home as he knew the kids would be asleep. He made me feel so guilty, but at the same time, and I think for the first time, I realized how much I had been doing for him at my own expense and vowed that from then on there would be more time for 'me.'

❋   ❋   ❋

One Master Warrant Officer's wife said she was 'tired of doing it all.' They needed a new car, but for once she was going to do nothing except pick out the colour. She wanted her husband to negotiate the deal, decide on the make of car, etc. So far she had been holding out for two months, determined to let the old car 'bottom out' in the driveway— she was adamant that she would not budge . . .

The Geographical Cure

I have resented my husband being in the Canadian Armed Forces for a number of reasons:

1. His alcohol problem. I became part of the problem by escapism. I went to bingo two or three times a week. I pretended the problem did not exist, or that I could wish it away. His drinking affected our finances, family, friends, social and sex life. It got so I hated for him to touch me. When he was sober, he was a saint, when drinking, a devil. I actually loved him as a person but hated his behaviour. I resented him for spoiling my social life and preventing me from making real friends.

2. I resented the military for regularly giving us the so-called 'geographical cure.' Of course my husband would promise to 'stop' drinking every time we were posted. But he was too sick to keep any promise. In fact I too became emotionally sick, as well as my children.

3. My husband's boss and a close friend knew he had a drinking problem, but covered up for him. They simply made the problem worse. No wonder I was heartsick, lonely and on the verge of a nervous breakdown. Fortunately, Al Anon came to my rescue and I feel as if I swallowed sunshine. My husband is in AA and my children go to Al Anon—a miracle!

Christmas

One of the happiest and yet saddest times of year for me is Christmas! Although I enjoy the season immensely, it always produces mixed emotions. The realization that we are so far from family is always magnified at this time of year. And for me, it has definitely been a disadvantage of this lifestyle. But for every negative there is a positive, and I can't tell you how excited I get when the mailman comes. I love to receive those Christmas cards and letters from friends and relatives all over the world, to catch up on their news, to hear what's new in their lives as well as their children's. The realization that, even though distance separates us all, we are remembered at this time of year creates its own closeness.

My son's girlfriend has lived in the same house all her life and spends a very busy holiday season with her family and relatives—most of whom live close by. So there is no need for them to send a card of greeting when they can greet each other personally. She was amazed at the number of Christmas cards we receive, whereas we more or less take it for granted.

The times when we are able to be with our families are precious. Take advantage of it while you can. As one woman told me, "As I packed away our Christmas ornaments this year, I wondered where I would be unpacking them next year . . ."

The Fun Side

Life as a military wife definitely does have its humorous side, as evidenced by the following comments:

> *For a tea party for my birthday we wore long gloves, big hats and sneakers. We got the tea cups out and there was sherry in the teapot.*

❋   ❋   ❋

> *The crazy things you do! A friend (Betty) lived a few houses up the street from us and she had picked up an attractive piece of driftwood at the shore. She wanted to put it on her*

front lawn but was afraid kids would take it—so she put it out front but close to the house by the living-room window. One early evening, just for fun, I decided to steal it with the help of another neighbour. It was difficult because Betty's inside front door was open and they were in the living room watching TV.

Another neighbour across the street was changing the light bulb outside his front door so we went over to him, told him what we were about to do and asked him not to put his light on until we were safely away with the driftwood. He and his wife invited us to come in for coffee when the 'dirty deed' was done. I managed to get the driftwood without being caught, but it was heavier than I expected and it was hard to run with it, as I was laughing so hard. So then my friend and I went struggling into the neighbour's house, complete with driftwood, to have our coffee. I got it home that night and put it on my front lawn (it was completely dark by then). Next I put a big sign on it—'For Sail,' as Betty's husband was Navy (we were Army). I knew Betty had to drive past my house to go bowling the next morning, so I was sure she would see it. The funny thing was that Betty loved it, but her friend, who only knew me slightly, took the whole thing seriously and thought I had some nerve to not only steal the driftwood but to turn around and try to sell it.

I decided to have lunch for the wives in the Squadron on a Saturday when the husbands would be home and they could babysit. I planned the menu (including Turkey à la King for 23 people) and household chores well in advance. My husband was away all week so I was on my own.

On Thursday I baked my turkey and had my dessert ready. On Friday I cut up the turkey and made the 'à la King.' Friday afternoon I had a hair appointment; Friday night I set the table. Saturday morning I took the Turkey à la King out of the fridge as the ladies were coming at 12:00 noon. Removing the lid from the pot, I discovered to my horror that the sauce had spoiled! I tried to heat it up to see if it would be OK. It was no good. I got a neighbour to come over to tell me what I had

done wrong. *She said I'd poison everyone!! Then she gave me*
a recipe for tuna casserole for 20-25 people.

I had to drive to the store and on my way encountered a
parade. Never before has my car driven over a ball diamond
but it did that day! As it turned out, my neighbour made two
casseroles for me and they were delicious. One friend, on
hearing about this, said, "How did you keep out of the sherry
bottle?"

The Serious Side

A significant part of being a military wife is the experience of standing
on the sidelines and watching your husband trying to deal with certain
aspects of his career:

It was 1968. My husband was on the plane when the guys
were doing a night jump, and several men parachuted in the
Ottawa River and drowned. I had to live through the whole
night before I found out that my husband was safe, but he had
lost all his close buddies. It was just terrible. I felt sadness at
this great loss and yet I also felt guilty because my husband
was alive! It was an agonizing experience for everyone.

Two months later the unit arranged a confidence jump. It
was important for the guys to jump again—for themselves and
for their friends. Some guys couldn't jump, but others did. On
this particular jump, Foymount was the drop zone and the fam-
ilies were included. They made a family day out of it, with
food, games for the kids, etc. It was a kind of healing process.
I remember looking up at the sky and watching the paratroop-
ers coming in for a landing. Everyone was totally committed
to everyone else there that day—a closeness that is beyond
description.

My husband spent two years as a career manager. Until that
time I thought all career managers played 'dart games' and
twiddled their thumbs. However, I no longer speak from a

position of ignorance. I watched my husband agonize over other people's problems, and there were times when the decision he made was not the one the family wanted. One has to remember that they are career managers, not social workers. Their job is to find the best solution for the forces as well as the individual.

Lonely at the Top

Is it really lonely at the top? Do the senior officers' wives really 'have it made'? These are some of the questions I posed to many wives in that position.

Everything is not always as it appears, and life as a senior officer's wife is no exception. Torn between wanting to support her husband in his career and wanting to be accepted for herself and have a career of her own, it is the senior officer's wife who seems to sacrifice the most. The majority of these wives who spoke with me were either teachers or nurses, but there were other professionals as well. The biggest complaint from the teachers, of course, is trying to work in the province you happen to be in at the time. With different qualifications required for each province, sometimes this can be really difficult.

I finally got my Ontario teaching certificate after four postings to Ottawa. But what good is it going to do me now, as we are posted out of the province!

Yes, I am treated differently now that my husband is a Commanding Officer. I worked with a grade 5 class for a month. Another woman had a grade 3 class—her husband was a Corporal. We really enjoyed each other's company. But she was so surprised when she found out what rank my husband was, she stayed away after that . . .

I would have stayed in nursing if I had not gotten into the military life. But if I had, I would never have discovered the Arts.

As a teacher in Cold Lake I had to live on the base and was a member of the Mess. Getting married was a step down, in that I was not allowed into the mess without my husband, and in that I could not work, because the Junior NCO's wives needed the money more . . .

I was a good student in high school and I think I could have gone places with my career—maybe Vice Principal, but that is not possible because of the lifestyle I have chosen.

Sometimes the responsibilities that go with this position can be overwhelming. If you are not basically an outgoing, 'people' person, the endless social functions can be very difficult.

The military system expects you to accompany your husband on posting (sometimes he won't get the job unless you do), expects you to entertain, expects you to head various committees—so much is expected of you that many wives feel they have no life of their own.

As a CO's wife people defer to me now. They expect me to be a leader because my husband is, but I have a life apart from the military!

I do not like expectations placed on me. It's a drag to entertain sometimes because they are my husband's associates and they are only there because of who my husband is. I like to entertain for my friends, but otherwise it's a chore.

I go to every function and parade my husband is in. I not only find it rewarding, but I feel it's part of my job as a CO's wife.

At my husband's Change of Command parade I was very nervous and didn't want to get out of the car that delivered me to the parade area. I was worried about tripping and knowing everyone would be watching . . .

Now that my husband has a senior position, I am more lonely than I ever was!

Whether you are a Private's wife or a General's wife, life in the military atmosphere creates a variety of problems, depending on the rank of your husband. The many conversations I have had with the wives leads me to think some of the misconceptions we have about each other are due to simply not understanding how 'the other half' lives. Yes, officers' wives do have a more social life and get to travel perhaps more than the wives of enlisted men. Their husbands also have bigger mess bills! They are also posted more often (every 2 years) which makes moving more difficult for the children, makes it much more difficult to adopt children, and makes it more difficult to establish friendships. When they do make friends, the question is constantly there—"Is she really my friend, or is she friendly with me because of who my husband is? You really don't know who to trust."

While the enlisted man's wife might not have to deal with the same problems, she perhaps has difficulties because money is tighter, and the opportunities for jobs for the military wife are not always readily available. She quite often has less understanding of the military lifestyle and therefore is less content. It's not a perfect lifestyle for either group.

Comments for the World

I would like to leave all of you non-military readers with comments from many wives when asked, "As a military wife, what do you want the world to know?"

That military wives should be treated like people, like individuals. We need a life too! I did not sign a contract with the military.

We are just as talented, independent and smart as any other group. Society in general thinks the military are all rejects from society and this is not so!

For the man it's a job. He enjoys his job and he loves his family. When he goes away, it is not personal.

The fact that you hear stories or rumours about military wives and teenagers being 'easy' doesn't mean it's all of us. A few bad apples spoil the reputation of us all and I resent it!

Just how hard it is not to have your husband come home at 5 p.m. every day. Not knowing where he is sometimes.

How dedicated our husbands are. To them it's not just a job— it's much more than that.

It is a lifestyle all its own. I want people to understand that there is no other profession to compare it with. There are other jobs where you have to be relocated, but it's not the same.

Anyone can be a civilian, but it takes special people to be part of the military community.

Chapter 5

Home Is Where the Military Sends Us

You know how lots of people have pillows with 'Home Sweet Home' on them. Well, I made some for the house—only they say: "Home Is Where the Army Sends Us!"

For those of us who move from one house to another every few years, we are continually called upon to make that house into a home—whether it be an actual house, a small apartment, or mansion.

In the early years of marriage, moving to a new location and accepting the challenges the move represents can be truly exciting. This job doesn't take any special talent—just a willingness to make that little extra effort over and above sticking furniture in each room. It's surprising how quickly you can adapt to your new surroundings when you've decorated your new place with many of your favourite things.

Civilians tend to think that because you are posted to their particular town or city that you should love it as they do, forgetting that we do have our own hometowns or adopted ones that we love. I think only someone from Grand Centre, Alberta could love Grand Centre, Alberta. I was born in Ottawa but have lived there only four years. I have adopted Vancouver as my hometown, as my family is there. Home really is where the heart is.

PMQs

For those of us who travel this countryside, trying to make yet another place into 'home,' the challenges are often very exciting. I have always enjoyed the excitement of wondering what our next place will be like, and the challenge of making another house into a home. But in the early years of our marriage it was more exciting than later on. By then there were children to consider, and finding a new place to live was more difficult because there were many extra considerations—like the proximity of schools to where we would live, how far away from the base the house was, could we both work with only one vehicle, etc. But in those early years when we went from base to base and moved into PMQs (Permanent Married Quarters), life was much easier. We had some good neighbours and some bad ones but, unlike civilian housing, we knew that if we were not exactly ecstatic about our new accommodations, in a few years we would be moving on to a different location. So we could always make the best of it for the time required.

I always loved living in PMQs. It was a very secure environment in many ways. Perhaps it gave us an attitude of 'us against them,' but I was always thankful to raise our son in that environment. He was born at a very busy time in my husband's career and I think it made us closer.

Two-Dollar Bills

So many times in my travels around the Petawawa area to do personal interviews, the following story appeared in various forms, and the version printed here appears to be the most popular one. It was a good lesson learned and I applaud the originator of the idea.

Around 1962 housing in Petawawa and surrounding areas was very difficult to find, as civilians were quite unwilling to rent to the military. At that time, the Base Commander (tired of the civilian community always knocking the military and the service members complaining about the frustrations of trying to find suitable accommodations for their families) decided to show the local population just how much they depended on the military for their economic survival.

With no advance explanation or warning, the Military Pay Office paid the entire base in two-dollar bills. Once the local areas were flooded with these bills, it didn't take long before they 'got the message.' By then it was quite obvious how much the military supported the local economy. It also showed the local merchants what they would lose if the military suddenly packed up and left the area.

I understand that as a result of this not-so-subtle reminder, the civilian community settled down and there were considerably fewer problems of this nature.

Security

Living in PMQs is such a secure life that you don't fully realize it until you leave them. When I look back, I think we were very fortunate to have been able to live in them. Yes, people complain about how slow CE is in making necessary repairs and how much we feel like sardines at times. For some, being in the military atmosphere 24 hours a day is hard to take. But when we branched out on our own it was a little scary, after living in PMQs for about 10 years.

Our house had a carport attached to it and we decided we'd like to close it in and install a garage door. My husband was away on course—back to where we had just been posted from about six months before (typical). I decided to get some estimates on what the job would cost so that my husband could make the decision when he got home and work could start quickly.

The third estimate appeared to be the most reasonable, so I told the fellow my husband was away for a month but we would get back to him with a 'yes' or 'no' as soon after that as we could. Later on that day it suddenly hit me that I was no longer in PMQs and should be more careful who I told that my husband was away!

In the PMQ setting you talk openly about being alone or your husband being away, because chances are many of your neighbours are in the same boat. But once you leave the PMQ atmosphere, it's another story.

Harassing Phone Calls

One of the hazards of this lifestyle is the availability of information on when units are away from home. With some exercises held at approximately the same time every year for different units/bases, it's not hard to find out when a certain unit will be away.

This situation can leave the wives vulnerable to unwanted telephone calls, and many wives have experienced obscene or harassing phone calls. At a time when many young wives are adjusting to military life, to being alone, to being lonesome, these phone calls can be very difficult to handle. But they are just as upsetting to any woman whose husband is away.

Many times the originator of these calls is someone from the husband's unit. Someone who knows the men are away and when they will be home. Someone who perhaps has a grudge against another unit member. These calls also happen when just the husband is away as opposed to the unit as a whole. It can happen at any time and is extremely upsetting for the receiver of the calls.

Because of the frequency with which this problem surfaced in my research, I felt it important not only to mention it here, but to offer some advice for anyone who might be experiencing such calls. According to military police sources, the best course of action is to immediately hang up. Do not converse with the caller. Then call the police. If necessary, the police may be able to temporarily install a trace telephone—one which records the phone number of the caller—or you can purchase one of these telephones. Many areas serviced by Bell Canada now have access to services such as *Call Screen* and *Call Trace*. With these new features, a voice announcement will inform you of the last number to call your number when a special code is dialed. There is a nominal fee charged for this service. Check the *Calling Features* pages in the front of your phone book, or call your local telephone company for details.

Another option is to change your telephone number. However, we shouldn't have to do that. We are only in one place for such a short time, and it takes time to build up a network of friends and acquaintances; changing your phone number can make it inconvenient and frustrating not only for the wife who is dealing with these calls, but for the whole family.

Ladies, if you are experiencing any problem of this nature, do not try to deal with it yourself. There are people out there who can help, and while it might take time to solve the problem, don't hesitate to ask for help. You don't have to put up with it!

Home Away from Home

Being so far away from home and relatives, those in the military community quickly form a bond. They help where help is needed.

> *On our street all the husbands were gone on UN taskings except one. He was just great helping us all wherever he could whether it was a car that wouldn't start or a lawn mower that just quit. His wife was a 'gem' for sharing him with us.*

It's not uncommon for neighbours away on vacation to come home to newly mowed grass or a driveway that's recently been cleared of a mountain of snow. People look out for each other.

I recall one amusing incident a few years ago in North Bay. My son and I were there trying to find a place for him to live while he attended college. A young single man around 27 years old had bought half of a duplex in a new subdivision and was renting out three bedrooms to students. We went to have a look and talk to him. When we arrived, he and his mother were busy unpacking and hanging curtains. The arrangement suited everyone fine, and we continued having a friendly discussion about the house and neighbourhood.

The young man commented with some concern that the woman in the other half of the duplex had already mowed his lawn earlier in the week before he started moving in. He seemed a little uneasy about this gesture and wondered how 'friendly' this neighbour was going to be. I immediately commented, "I'll bet her husband is in the military!" I was right, and the young man was completely surprised that I would know that, because nothing in his conversation had referred to the husband's employment.

I went on to explain to him and his mother that in the military community it was the neighbourly thing to do. We help where we can. You don't need to know someone to offer a helping hand, and you look out for each other. What this military wife did would have been immediately accepted and appreciated within the military community. In the civilian community, her motives were questionable!

Since 'home' for us can mean 101 different places, the times when we are able to travel to our original 'home' and be with family and relatives are always special. But there is one thing that many wives have complained about:

We are the only ones away from home and I get tired of us always being the ones to do the travelling. It's no farther for my family to come to where we live, but they always just sit and wait for us to do the travelling. Then once we are home, everyone expects us to visit them instead of them realizing how much we have travelled and come to visit us where we are staying . . .

Buying a House Alone

Having your husband away when it's time to move is nothing new to many wives. Buying a house on your own is a tremendous responsibility, but time and time again military wives prove to themselves and others just how capable and versatile they really are:

My husband was in Somalia and we were posted to Ottawa a week after he was due to return. We had decided to buy a house (our first) but I would have to do it alone. My husband usually handles the finances. I had never done a budget, but I did one before he left for Somalia so that I knew how much we spent each month.

I approached this venture of buying a house like a course and felt I would pass the course if I bought a house successfully. I followed the steps outlined in a book I got from the library. I researched the area we wanted to live in, and narrowed it down to a few houses. It was at this point that I became overwhelmed. I was tempted to reach my husband in Somalia and ask him to come home and help me buy the house. But I knew that he would defer to me because he would want me to be happy with the house, so then I realized I could do it myself and I was OK.

If my husband had not been away, I would never have learned how to do this on my own. Certainly if he was not in the military I probably would never have become involved in buying a house at all. It was a big experience for me, and one that makes me proud of my accomplishment. My husband was very pleased and proud of my doing it on my own.

Chapter 6

Ankle Biters, Rug Rats and House Apes

When our first son was about a year old, we went to an Engineer parade celebrating the Unit's birthday. We met several friends, and one young single fellow asked us where our 'rug rat' was. I had no idea what he was referring to until my husband pointed to our son in his stroller in the shade of a nearby tree. I was very hurt at this casual, uncalled-for reference to our precious child and made up my mind that this fellow might be a friend of my husband's but he was no friend of mine! However, I soon learned that the terminology used in this lifestyle requires a strong sense of humour. So if you are inclined to take everything seriously, as I was, you may have to 'lighten up' considerably. How else would I and many other wives have been able to survive the various labels placed on us from the love of our life—'The Warden' (in my absence); 'My loving wife' (in my presence); 'My 2IC'; 'the old woman'; etc.

What is it like bringing up children in a military atmosphere? For some parents it is more difficult than others, just as some children adjust more easily to the lifestyle. With my husband in a field unit and continually away, for me it meant having one son withdraw into himself while the other literally sobbed his heart out in my arms every time their father went away. I can remember many trips to the Base when the boys were young to drop my husband off as he was leaving 'again,' with the boys and I crying all the way home. But after a few days, the boys always seemed to turn to each other for comfort. And to this day they are extremely close although very different in personalities; in fact, over the years, people have often commented on their closeness. I believe that although the lifestyle was difficult for them in that their father was constantly away, it has given them a closeness that they might not have found had their lives been spent in a civilian atmosphere.

I tried to make special times with the children while their father was away—like having TV dinners in front of the TV, something we didn't do when my husband was home. It was to be 'our secret—we won't tell Dad!' Of course, invariably the first thing Dad heard on his return was "We had TV dinners while you were gone and we didn't even sit at the table!"

❋ ❋ ❋

Many times the wives told me stories of how their boyfriends, husbands and brothers in uniform were mistaken for some other person — a commissionaire, a waiter, a porter, etc. While I am sure there were times when the men didn't appreciate the humour of the mistake, in retrospect you really do have to laugh.

My two eldest children were 3 and 4 when my husband joined the service. They had no idea of rank in those days and alternately told folks their Dad was a general or a mailman.

I am the product of a military family. My father was in the Army for 26 years. Ironically, all three of us children were born in Pembroke, Ontario, at the Cottage Hospital. The Petawawa posting for us was the longest and to this day I still dearly love the place, and have many fond memories from there.

I may not have married military, but I often wished that I had, as there has always been something missing from my life. The service families are different from civilians. They had to help one another out more than regular civilians.

There is one memory that I would like to share with you. We were living on Brock Square just off Dundonald Drive. I believe my age to have been somewhere between 6 and 9. The men had been out in the area for quite a while and when they came home it was like a parade. The vehicles all drove down Dundonald Drive in a convoy. I recall seeing all the wives and children standing along the street waving to the men upon their return, each one looking for their father or husband. This was something that I never, ever forgot in all the years I have been away. It was special. My heart still soars, remembering that, as I was one of the kids looking for her father.

At family gatherings I really feel like we are outsiders even though it's all our family. All the other children live close together so they know each other well, but it's hard for my kids because they are more like strangers.

I tried to keep my husband a part of conversations and encouraged the children to write their father. Phone calls were great

*but when they were over, they were over; you could re-read
letters as many times as you wanted.*

Today, with the advent of videos, it's so much easier to keep Dad a
somewhat visible presence. It also enables Dad to still feel a part of the
family and experience the changes—particularly in very young children
who grow so fast. Videos are also an excellent way of bridging the gap
between grandparents and other relatives, although it isn't the same as
kissing, hugging and talking . . .

Not Me

No matter in what atmosphere you bring your children up, I'm sure all of
you have at one time or another found a 'Not Me' in your house . . .

As far back as I can remember, 'Not Me' was always a part of my
life. In a way, I guess you could say he has been a steady, reliable, constant, sometimes frustrating, invisible companion.

From childhood, through high school, sharing an apartment with my
cousin, being married, having children, etc., 'Not Me' has always been
there. I suspect when the boys have left home and started on the next
phase of their adult lives, 'Not Me' will still be with us—like a good old
faithful dog.

Sometimes he has been described as extremely forgetful—like that
time in the hot, hot summer when I watched the garbage truck whiz by
our house without stopping. "Whose turn was it to put the garbage out?"
I yelled. The reply—"Not Me!" He could also be described as having a
knack for doing or not doing things at the wrong time. Whenever things
weren't done, it was always 'Not Me' who was guilty. When things
weren't done right, like leaving the house with the TV and lights still on,
invariably 'Not Me' was at it again.

He seems to take delight in having the stereo going full blast, leaving the lawn mower out in the rain, forgetting to put the jam and peanut
butter away and forever leaving a ring around the bathtub! And as frustrated as I get at times, I know 'Not Me' will always be there. If I have
any doubts, all I have to do is ask a question and invariably someone
will tell me 'Not Me' is the culprit once again.

Even the boys have always included 'Not Me' in their daily routine.

In fact, he has always played a big part in their activities and is constantly on their minds. One time the boys were late for supper and I was
really worried; both boys felt bad having to blame 'Not Me,' as it was
his turn to check the time.

However, don't get me wrong; 'Not Me' isn't always into mischief.
Take the time I found a lovely box of chocolates under the Christmas
tree. When I asked hubby and the boys who put them there, they all
responded in unison—"Not Me." So he can be quite a thoughtful character as well. I also remember receiving a lovely flower arrangement at
work from "A Secret Admirer." Again, 'Not Me' was being nice to me.

So if 'Not Me' ever pays a visit to your house and decides to show
his frustrating, forgetful side—don't be too hard on him. If you are
patient enough, eventually this shy, mischievous, caring character will
show you that he is anything but one-dimensional. Keeping you guess-
ing what he'll be up to next is all part of his charm. I wouldn't have him
any other way!

Having Children

For some families who have definite thoughts on how many children
they would like to have and how far apart they want to have them, the
military lifestyle does not always agree—even when Mother Nature is
willing to cooperate.

> *This would be a good time for us to have another child, except
> that he is going to be away for 12 months! I don't want to
> have another child alone . . .*

> *We wanted our children two years apart but that all went out
> the window this year. Having a baby is just not one of those
> things you can accomplish when you and your husband are
> thousands of miles apart!*

❋   ❋   ❋

Likewise, adoption for military families is much more frustrating
and sometimes impossible. This mobile lifestyle doesn't always leave

couples in one province long enough to complete the adoption process, even if time has allowed the process to begin. As requirements differ from province to province, many military couples find themselves 'that close' to having that much wanted child, only to be posted away and facing the heartbreaking decision to start all over . . .

What's for Supper?

With all growing children, "What's for supper?" is one of the most often heard phrases. Sometimes there is a quick ready answer, but other times the question evokes a growling reaction. As a working mother, that phrase was always music to my ears on the days that I was at home. It was a time to review the day's happenings with the children while they negotiated a peanut butter and jelly sandwich to tide them over until supper.

However, there were many times when my response was, "Do we have to eat again today?" Sometimes trying to come up with a different meal seems just too much to handle, especially when you are working outside the home and are pressed for time.

With the introduction of microwaves as another of the must-have luxury items, life has been made much simpler for the working mother. I can remember the novelty of our microwave and the kids sitting watching the hot dogs go round and round on the turntable. I swear the first few weeks we had that machine I fed the entire neighbourhood hot dogs—"Hi, Jake, come see our new microwave—want a hot dog?"

Next time you feel like a night off from the rigours of the hot stove and impatient, hungry children, just issue kitchen vouchers—good for one do-it-yourself microwaveable meal—and then slink into a nice hot bubble bath. With a little luck someone might feel sorry for you and cook you a hot dog too!

Daddy's Gone

Plans must often change when Dad's job needs him elsewhere.

It's so hard when the guys are away. I remember one time my 10-year-old son's hockey team was having a skate-a-thon to raise money for the team. As usual, my husband was away. I didn't feel right about asking my friends and co-workers to support my son. It was his responsibility to get sponsors. However, I did ask my friends to sponsor me and decided I would skate with the boys. On the day of the event I found myself the only parent on the ice. I hadn't been on skates for a few years and I kept catching the pick of my skates on the ice and falling. I soon had a following of my son's teammates skating with me, waiting to pick me up when I fell.

In the time allotted for his group, I had circled the rink 86 times. The next day my right elbow was swollen bigger than my knee. I guess I kept hitting it when I fell down. It took days before it was back to normal. You know, the only comment my son made about that day was that his Dad wasn't there to watch him . . .

In late spring when the kids were about 2 and 5, we bought a brand new tent trailer complete with 8 x 10 add-a-room, and we were all looking forward to a whole summer of camping. My husband is the outdoor type and was so excited about teaching the kids more about nature. A week after we got the trailer, he was assigned to teach first aid to the militia all summer. That meant he would be out in the area staying in a tent

with the militia all week and only home on weekends! How could I expect him to go camping with us on the weekends when that was what he had been doing all week? The summer was a write-off!

With Dads away so much, many is the time the Moms feel like they need to split themselves into several pieces. It can be especially hard when you have several children participating in a variety of activities. You can't be in two places at once, and at times like these the older children sometimes lose out as the younger ones can't travel on their own. The older ones are asked to travel with the network of Moms in the same situation. But as difficult as it can be deciding whose event you attend this week, and whose you'll miss, the agony of not being there when your child accomplishes something, whether it's a strike in bowling or a goal in hockey, is deeply felt.

I tried so hard to be Father and Mother when my husband was away. I had a full-time job and each summer and winter it seems the weekends were taken up with taking the boys to hockey, baseball or soccer. We just seemed to have a short breather between sports. One of the things I always felt bad about was the special events I missed. Yet I was certainly there for the boys more than my husband, and it was really upsetting for him only hearing about these special times.

One time both boys had a ball tournament on the same weekend about 10 miles from our home. They were playing in different areas, so I knew it was going to be rough going from field to field and that I would no doubt be spending the whole day at one field or the other. We watched most of my younger (aged 7) son's game until it was time to take my older son (aged 10) to his field. They were behind schedule there so I left him and hurried back to see the rest of my seven-year-old's game. Just as I rounded the corner of the school from the parking lot I heard a lot of cheering and as I got nearer I saw my son running from third to home. He had hit a grand slam! His first words to me were "You didn't see it, did you

Mom!" I thought of lying to him to make him feel better but I knew there would be other times when I or his father wouldn't 'be there' so I was honest, as much as it hurt us both. I did try to stress the crowd's cheering him on and that I did see him cross home plate. But we both knew that it was hitting the ball that was the most important thing to him—the grand slam was secondary!

Education

The emotional upheaval created when Dad goes away can surface in many ways. More than one child has had difficulties in school, and the wise teacher dealing with military children who reads the following story will perhaps begin by asking, "Is your Dad away?" if a child's work suddenly changes.

When our youngest was in grade two I attended a parent/teacher interview and discovered that he was doing really well in school up to a point and then all of a sudden his school work was way down—the difference between night and day. I couldn't understand what was happening and it took the teacher and me quite a while exploring different theories

before we realized that the time his work started to decline was when my husband went away. As soon as he returned, our son's school work was back to normal. Every time my husband went away the same thing would happen. I began sending a note to let the teacher know when my husband was going away and for how long, so she would understand if there was another sudden change in his school work. For several years after that I would discuss this problem with his teacher at the start of every year and continue to send notes to school letting her know when my husband would be away.

However, many mothers commented on the educational positives of this lifestyle:

My son is in grade 2 and he knows all the provinces and their capitals—most kids his age only know a few. But he has lived in four of those capitals already.

Our kids are so much more knowledgeable than their civilian friends. I can remember when we came here and drove through Thunder Bay. One of my daughters was seven at the time and she remembered Terry Fox and the fact that he took ill in Thunder Bay and was unable to finish the run. We saw the statue erected in his honour and understood the significance of it, and she will always remember that. But most kids will never get to see that statue—all they remember is what they hear every year during the Terry Fox Run.

Daddy?

An incident that surfaced in many different forms throughout the interviews was the embarrasing moment many wives faced when their young children called the first person they saw in uniform 'Daddy!' (invariably the real Daddy was away at the time).

For me one of those moments was in 1967, when I was shopping at the MLS (now Canex) in Werl, Germany. My son, sitting in the grocery cart, put his arms out and called "Da! Da!" to a soldier walking towards us. He stopped, looked me up and down and replied "Sorry son, I'm not your Daddy, but I wish I was . . ." I felt my face turn the same colour as my slacks—red!

With Daddy away so much in the young children's lives, no wonder they get confused and, considering they see him in uniform more times than not, anyone can be fair game!

Chapter 7

Teen Talk

Our teens go through a variety of emotions handling this gypsy lifestyle. One quarter of those questioned objected to being labelled a 'military brat.' They felt they were no different from any other teens except they moved every few years.

Of those who responded, there was almost an equal number of guys and girls, the guys having a slight lead. Their ages ranged from 9 to 21 years, with 17 being the average age. Their father's rank ranged from Corporal to Lieutenant Colonel, and half of them came from families with two children.

I asked all these young adults what the hardest adjustment for them was in moving from place to place. Without a doubt, leaving friends is the biggest concern, closely followed by making new friends and adjusting to new schools. But many teens had suggestions for making the moves easier.

For Their Peers:

Just take a deep breath, say 'here we go again' and don't have a closed mind about the new place.

Definitely write to your old friends but try and make new friends soon.

Learn as much as you can ahead of time about your new posting.

Allow yourself to be open and try not to be shy.

Try and make the best of every place.

Be yourself, don't try and impress the people you meet.

Once you have been posted, immediately enroll in some kind of sport.

Don't get too close to people!

How sad to see that even some teens feel the need to build that invisible wall around their emotions. Why? Because they find it extremely difficult to leave their present environment to face the 'unknown.' Their reasoning—if you don't get too close to people then you won't have to disentangle yourself emotionally when it comes time to leave . . .

Just think how hard some of us adults find the constant moving: for some teens it's 10 times worse. If they get into the habit of 'building that wall' as young teens, by the time they become adults it can be very difficult to penetrate.

When I was in Nova Scotia for a visit I was a total outcast. They almost wouldn't talk with me at all. (age 16)

Loneliness

It lurks around every corner,
It knows you are not expecting it,
It is stalking you;
For you are its prey.
Day or night it will haunt you
It may strike . . .
At any time . . .

—Krista Gilby (age 13)

As military parents we must ensure that we support our children fully throughout their growing years and not just 'assume' they will tag along and cope adequately with each move.

For the System:

Have a good teen centre at every base.

Have one federal school system.

Let it be the family's decision to move, not the military's.

Make the postings longer.

Although that sounds like a good idea, experience has shown the longer the posting is the more difficult it is to leave friends behind—it makes the move harder, not easier.

It would be easier if there was an information pamphlet just for teens.

This is an excellent idea and one that I feel should definitely be implemented. However, in order for it to be successful, it must be designed and produced by teens. Our young adults will have more faith in the accuracy of something that is prepared by their peers. This venture not only would be a way for the teens to participate in the moving process, but would probably help alleviate some of the concerns teens have about moving to a strange place.

Of all the responses, there were two young women who went into much more detail in their replies, which offer excellent advice:

I'm just as guilty of this as anyone, but constant comparison of the new location to the past posting can be deadly! My last move (to Edmonton) from Borden after 4+ years was the hardest for me (then 16 years old). All I did was sit in the house, mope, cling to memories and wish I were back 'home.' It destroyed any chance of making friends and made me miserable. I did go back to Borden, just to find things had changed just as much there (everyone was gone). It sent me 'home' realizing Alberta wasn't so bad after all. (age 18)

Keep in touch with old friends (good friends will remain good friends) but remember that life goes on—in other words, get out and meet new people, get involved at school or in the community. Try not to think about your friends too much during the 'critical' period (right after the move—how long depends on the individual). Thinking about your friends 'back home' right after you move will keep you in the past; you will not enjoy your new life and talking about your friends may alienate you (the new people you meet will get tired of hearing you talking about friends 'back home'). Enjoy your new friends, appreciate them. Once you're settled in it's fine to look back fondly, but beware at first. Remember that you won't always be miserable. You will get over it soon and in no time you'll be looking back and saying, "Why was I worried about not fitting in?" (age 17)

Stress

As stress seems to play a part in all our lives at one time or another, I asked the group on a scale of 1-10 (with 10 being the highest) what they felt their stress level was in trying to adjust to a new posting. Sixty-six per cent rated their stress level 7 and above, with 20 per cent rating it at 10. Obviously our children have a difficult time moving and although the older they get the better the understanding, it doesn't decrease the apprehension of pulling up stakes and starting all over.

Many people think that army postings put a large stress on adolescents. I think that the only stress is to make new friends.

It usually depends on the compatibility of that individual. I know at our school we stick together and it is rare that we single anyone out or pick on people, for their father's rank especially. The only time one person is centred out is when their attitude conflicts. (age 16)

As difficult as moving might be for some, there are definite advantages to the lifestyle: meeting new people and seeing new places top the list.

I can't picture myself living in one place for more than a few years. It would get boring. (age 17)

School

But one third of the responses showed that the teens would have preferred to grow up and do their schooling all in the same place.

In every place I've been the schools are at different levels. If I stayed in one place I wouldn't have to adjust. (age 14)

The school systems wouldn't differ, [I would have] lasting friendships and contentment with surroundings. (age 18)

I wouldn't have had so much problems with the work in the different schools. (age 20)

Going through school with the same friends is easier than trying to adjust. (age 20)

One of the disadvantages to the lifestyle was being put back a grade when moving to a different province, and some teens had to deal with this more than once. Some turned bitter towards their parents because of it. This bitterness affected school performance, and problems at school then magnified. However, here is a wonderful success story:

I had so many problems when I was going to school because

we had moved to so many different ones that I quit when I had only done 3/4 of grade 9. I quit because I was afraid I would fail again. I had failed grades 3, 4 and 7. After about two years when my father was posted to Petawawa, I decided to go back to school. I am really glad I did. I'm doing a great deal better than I did before. I should be graduating next year. (age 20)

Of the provincial school systems themselves, there were almost as many answers showing Ontario as the hardest school system as there were claiming it to be the easiest. Since many factors come into play in determining an average answer to which is the most difficult/easiest system, suffice it to say that life would be much easier for our children if there was only one federal school system. That fact alone would tremendously ease the anxieties of teens on the move.

For teens as for adults, life does have its funny moments.

There was one incident on one of the MASH programs that really stayed with me. Hot Lips was explaining that she was a military brat and that she always thought a civilian was someone who was waiting for their uniform to come from the dry cleaners! I can relate to that!

One of my friends when we lived in Ottawa was a civilian. She thought everything was green and we lived in tanks . . . (age 17)

Being a 'military brat,' I can remember one incident that always brings a chuckle. I was in high school in Borden and our basketball team was playing some of the teams from the surrounding civilian schools. I was surprised that they knew so little about us. We used to tell them that on Mondays we washed the tanks, we cleaned the guns on Sunday and we all marched to school every day. We were just having fun, but they believed us!

Other teenagers from civilian schools think the biggest insult to a military brat is 'Your mother wears Army boots!' They also think we drive around in tanks, etc. (age 18)

Here in Petawawa we get called Army brats by the people who live in the village, who we call Village Idiots! (age 15)

In Germany my friends and I were called PMQ Brats. (age 18)

I made the cheerleading team two years ago at my high school and one of the others said jokingly to me, 'We'll have to get you a pair of runners 'cause you can't cheer in Army boots, you know!' (age 18)

When you talk to people who don't know the military way of life, they think that the kids have to have short haircuts and get passes to leave the base. (age 20)

On the family scene, most teens agreed that their father was the strongest disciplinarian (72%) while 84 per cent claimed to have a good relationship with their fathers whether they were away a great deal or not. Those fathers who discussed their jobs at home led by a slight margin over those who didn't, but the percentage of children who felt they understood just what their father's job was reached 75 per cent.

A small number felt their fathers didn't know what they were all about, while an equal number felt their fathers treated them like 'one of his men.' It is interesting that in most cases it was the same teens who responded negatively to both questions.

For all children, birthdays are important, and missing such an event is not only hard on Dad but harder still on the children. One 16-year-old boy said his father had missed seven birthdays, while one 16-year-old girl claimed eight birthdays celebrated without Dad. On the average, though, Dad seems to have been home for all but one or two of these special days.

Another problem that surfaced for some teens was dating. Many teens live in PMQs which are allotted according to rank, and the girls found this a disadvantage at times because when a fellow took them home, it was a dead giveaway as to their father's rank. Even in their teens, these young adults want to be accepted for themselves and not accepted or rejected because of who their father is. Still, more than one teen found their father's rank an advantage: "Attitudes change immediately when people recognize my last name or when people ask me who my father is . . ."

On the positive side of having a father who is an officer, the teens felt their parents could better afford tutors to help them if they were having problems adjusting to a new school system, whereas teens whose fathers were lower ranks and who didn't make as much money might not be able to afford tutoring for their children. But on the whole, most fathers impressed on their children not to 'use' their father's rank, whatever it was.

For some, the constant moving was very frustrating:

All it takes for me is one remark from a teacher labelling us 'military brats' and I just give up and quit trying . . .

While for others:

One group dreams of 'getting away' and seeing the world—the other group actually does it!

If you really don't like an area in which you are living, you can make do for now and look forward to moving somewhere else in a few years. This is a luxury our civilian counterparts don't have. (age 18)

Several teens added comments to the questionnaire over and above what I had asked for, which showed me that they not only took their involvement in this project seriously, but they unanimously stated, "It's about time someone asked us what we think!" Here are some sample comments:

You mean someone really wants to know what I think?

I can really say anything I want on this questionnaire?

I think your book will be very good because it will enable parents and family to make an easier transition if we know how other parents deal with the difficulties and problems in moving. (age 19)

Your project is interesting and it will show civilians that they are the same and that they aren't any better. (age 17)

I think it's good being asked for my opinion so adults will know what I think and feel about. (age 9!)

It will help civilians understand what the military goes through in moving. (age 18)

Thank you so much for caring about the teens and good luck with this worthwhile project. (age 18)

I asked the teens if they were planning on joining the military themselves. A strong 70 per cent said a definite NO! while 20 per cent were just as definite with their YES! The other 10 per cent were all 'MAYBEs' . . .

I know myself that I would never join the Army. As a kid, I never liked it and I wouldn't want to have to put my kids through it. Because someone is an 'army brat,' others who are not in the army (kids, etc.) may think differently of you. (age 17)

The military is an extremely difficult lifestyle, and I have not enjoyed moving around. The pressure is very high, and there are more problems as a result of this. My father is a 'great' father and has always tried to make our lives happy, but I would never choose the army as my career! (age 18)

❋   ❋   ❋

The teens themselves feel that, as a whole, their group is more ambitious because they are well travelled and don't fit into the same mould as those kids who are born and brought up in the same place.

One adult put it another way:

I asked my son what success meant to him and he said, being where I am, doing what I am doing, and not wanting to be anywhere else.

Chapter 8

The Helping Hand

There are various avenues available to assist today's military families in adjusting to, and living, this lifestyle. Military family resource centres, established at every base, offer a variety of services, including quality of life programs, information and referral, resume preparation, baby-sitting services, self-defence courses and a 24-hour crisis line, to name only a few.

Military Family Resource Centres

In April 1987 the Family Support Program Project (FSPP) was formed in Ottawa. Its purpose was to develop a policy (using a community format) for the Canadian Forces which would support military families. At last, the 'system' was recognizing that military wives and families do exist! No longer were we being looked on as 'excess baggage.' We were real, we had needs and concerns, and finally they were being addressed. No longer would we be told, "If the military had wanted the men to have a wife and family they would have issued them one!"

My first reaction to hearing that some sort of program would eventually be put into place was, "Great! Where were you 25 years ago?" Although this program would arrive too late for me, I was very excited about the difference it would make, especially for the young wives starting out in this lifestyle, and about the possibilities of this program. That excitement remains today.

As a result of the FSPP, in 1991 the Military Family Support Program was established. This meant that the Canadian Forces would establish resource centres on all military bases and funds would be set aside in Ottawa to implement them. Community Coordinator organizations would also be established at foreign locations where there was a large enough military family population to warrant it.

There is no need to elaborate on the problems associated with creating these centres, other than to mention a few:

- the reluctance of military personnel to accept the centres (Here we go babysitting the wife and kids! What next!)

- establishing the centres

- finding qualified staff

- adjusting the program to fit the different needs of each military base

- educating the families and the military on what the mandate for the centres is

Suffice it to say that, as with anything that is new and different, there are growing pains and adjustments. What I want to emphasize here is how every military wife can benefit from the centre and how important it is that you participate—as either a volunteer, a user, or a salaried employee.

At each centre there is a voluntary working board of directors which *must* consist of *at least* 51 per cent military spouses. Not military women, but the spouses of military personnel. As a board member, for the first time ever, *you* have a direct say in the planning of programs and the hiring of personnel. These centres are for *you!* In one sense, you could say you own them and you control their rate of growth.

This is a golden opportunity for all military wives and for their families. No longer do you have to sit back and just 'accept' whatever happens. You can participate in the formation of programs that meet *your* needs.

I urge you all to take a look at your centre. Find out who is on the board of directors. They should all be available to you. They represent each of you on the board and you should know who they are and what their interests in the centre are.

Each centre employs a director who handles the day-to-day administration. She/he answers to the board of directors. While board members' qualifications vary, they must all be prepared for a serious and active involvement with the board. The centre is only as strong as its board. If you are interested in participating as a board member, contact your centre, tell them of your interest and they will be able to advise you of any existing or upcoming vacancies.

If becoming a board member is not for you, then why not volunteer at the centre? There are many programs that depend on volunteers, from babysitting at the centre, to instructing a craft class or sharing your experiences with other wives on moving, bringing up children in this lifestyle, etc. Visit your local centre, introduce yourself and have a cup of coffee—you will soon learn what the centre in your area offers and where you can help. One advantage of volunteering or being employed at these centres is that even though you are posted every few years, you take your experiences and knowledge with you and hopefully the next resource centre will benefit.

You wives have a multitude of talents, and if you are not able to find a job in the area where you live, or if you just want to get out of the house for a few hours here and there, then please visit the centre—it could be a turning point for you. Lonely? Don't know many people? Then visit the centre. It's a great place to make new friends. Feel nervous alone at night? Would you be interested in a self-defence course? Then check with your centre and see if they offer one. If they don't, discuss it with them. The centre is there to serve you, and they don't know what you need unless you tell them.

Recently I visited with the Director, Military Family Support in Ottawa, LCol R. MacLellan, and I was impressed! Having spent my whole 'career' being made to feel by the system as though I really wasn't important, it was such a refreshing change to be in an atmosphere where military wives were number one. We are important and there are definitely people in the military who are there to help. I was impressed with the progress the whole system has made since its beginnings such a short time ago.

Until now the men have always come first; they have been the ones that 'counted.' But now, with the resource centres, *we* come first. Our time has finally come!

With the possibility of more UN taskings looming in the future, it is hoped that all centres will pull together with rear parties and women's groups to work diligently for the common good. At the same time I hope you ladies will realize just how lucky you really are to have such tremendous support available.

I have been a military spouse for over thirty years and while I agree that we (as military spouses) are unique and perhaps the largest group, we must not forget that there are many other groups of spouses out there, eg. RCMP, private sector companies such as the oil and hi-tech industry, external affairs and other large international corporations—all with families who are uprooted regularly and facing the same problems with schools, housing and out-of-country postings together with husbands who travel a great deal. We are fortunate to have the Family Support system in place. My sincere wish is that we instill in our young military wives a sense of pride in who they are and that they in turn will promote this pride to their children, husbands and fellow military friends.

The *Canadian Forces Personnel Newsletter*, in its Issue 6/93, was able to assert: "The MFSP has reached its goal of becoming a vital part of the military way of life to make the future brighter for military families and their community."

Rear Parties

As family contentment is finally being recognized as an integral part of what makes each serviceman perform to the best of his ability, the military has taken great strides in dealing with the everyday problems the family unit faces as our men leave home to fulfill their job requirements.

According to religious sources, those families who have religious beliefs have fewer problems while their husbands are away. Their faith sustains them, and they are better prepared to handle whatever difficulties might arise. One of the main concerns from the Padre's point of view is the lack of communication between soldiers and their spouses before a major tasking. Briefings held by unit personnel are open to soldiers and their families, and yet many families do not participate. "One wife could have had all her problems solved if she had attended a briefing beforehand. But she didn't, and thus she created more anxiety for herself and more work for the rear party."

When a UN tasking is to be carried out by a company or unit, a "rear party" is formed to stay behind and attend to any administrative work required by service members who have departed. It may be to answer queries concerning pay problems, or to assist in notifying and assisting with transportation when there has been a death in the immediate family, or to arrange briefings to the families, and newsletters and social functions to help keep family morale at an acceptable level.

From the wives' point of view, there are two types of rear parties. One employs the sick, lame or lazy who are not able to perform the tasking; the other has competent personnel remaining (mainly because the Commanding Officer sees the importance of a well-run rear party). However, this second group can and do show some resentment at being left to 'babysit hysterical wives and screaming kids' and they would much rather be with their peers on the tasking. Either way, the wives feel they lose out somewhat. However, in all fairness, I must point out that many women believe erroneously that the rear party's main function is to be at their beck and call. This is not correct. In the past, the women's general expectations of a rear party were quite often set way too high and sometimes resulted in their being critical of the help they received.

Calling the rear party and asking to have someone till your garden is totally unrealistic, as is expecting to have your driveway shovelled after every snowstorm when you are physically capable and/or have teens at home. But if you are alone and pregnant or have a medical problem that prevents you from engaging in strenuous physical activity, then support is usually provided. What the ladies have to bear in mind is the number of husbands away compared to the number of personnel in the rear party.

> *Sometimes I feel like I am a husband to 126 women, sitting across the table listening to all the problems (washer broke, car won't start, etc.) that they would share with their husbands. What they have to stop and realize is that there are 126 of them and only two of us!*

In future, what needs to be done is some standardization—both for rear parties and for the ladies' groups. Those running the rear parties need some definite guidelines as to what is expected of them by the military, particularly in dealing with the families. In the past, with several units on the same base away at the same time, services offered to the families by the rear parties differed from unit to unit. This led to some dissatisfaction amongst the wives, when one felt she was receiving less support than her neighbour, whose husband was from another unit.

Rear parties have to continually be aware of the emotional state the majority of the wives are in, trying to 'do it all' and deal with many mixed emotions at the same time. Their husbands are gone to a war-torn area for who knows how long. Media reports are not always accurate, so the only place the women can turn to for information, and to liaise with their husband's unit, is the rear party. Most of their families are no doubt thousands of miles away, and the wives rely heavily on support from the rear party. Patience, compassion and understanding will go a long way towards creating rapport with the wives and making everyone's life easier.

At the same time, the ladies have to ensure their expectations of the rear parties are realistic, and recognize just how lucky they are to have such an avenue open to them. This group is the link to your husband and for that you should count your blessings. Don't accept it as a 'given'—appreciate it as a godsend.

In the rear party staff I have observed, many go out of their way as well as give up a lot of their own free time to help the wives—using their own vehicles to deliver newsletters to each wife, going from door to door, working long hours to organize events for the wives, which are sometimes poorly attended. Regardless of why they were left behind to man the rear party, most take it as a serious commitment and endeavour to participate to the best of their ability.

Ladies' Groups

When the men are away on UN taskings, ladies within the unit gather together and form a working group. Their purpose is to liaise with the rear party, voice any concerns the wives might have, work with the rear party in arranging social functions and assist with newsletters. They develop a telephone network amongst themselves to ensure that no wife is left out and that she is in contact with another unit wife on a regular basis.

A few women whose husbands are in the lower ranks felt intimidated and looked down upon by members of the ladies' group. Remember that the higher the rank your husband has, the more knowledgeable you are about the military system—how it works, who the contact people are, etc. But women who are just starting out in this lifestyle are adjusting to many things and dealing with many emotions—some very new to them. They are frightened and scared and often feel all alone. For those of you who become involved in these ladies' groups, please do your utmost to include and encourage these young ladies to participate on your committees. It's through them that you will reach the majority of young wives. They will feel more comfortable dealing with the whole situation if they know their interests and concerns are really represented by their peers.

The women who do devote their time to these groups have no experience or qualifications for what they are doing. They become involved because they have a genuine interest in helping, have free time to contribute or feel their participation is an obligation because of their husband's position. They are jumping in with both feet and doing their best to help. Remember, their husbands are away also and they have children and responsibilities at home. They are also going through the same emotional upheavals you are.

✳   ✳   ✳

I want to assure the wives that the military is well aware of how difficult a time it can be when your husband is on a UN tasking and I feel very confident that with any future taskings, every effort will be made to ensure that assistance is available to help you deal with this difficult time.

We must not forget the men who are away. Anxiety is not restricted to the wives and children. The men need to know that their families left behind are not 'adrift and at sea.'

With the Family Resource Centres, rear parties and ladies' groups, more support is available to the wives than ever before. Every group must do their utmost to band together to make the difficult times as smooth-running as possible for everyone. Every member of our 'family' is equally important.

Chapter 9

On the Road Again

O n the road again, I just can't wait to get on the road again . . ."
Willie Nelson must surely have been thinking about military
families when he recorded that popular song. Before the moving comes the long awaited or completely surprising 'posting message'
advising the service member that he is about to be transferred to another
location. Sometimes there is a further suspenseful wait to find out the
date of the actual move. But whether it's a much awaited posting or a
complete surprise, many families can see themselves in the following
article by Connie Bowers.

Posted

It is the best of times, it is the worst of times. It is a time of
elation, it is a time of deflation. It is hello time, it is goodbye
time. It is posting time. I have discovered, through the past
number of years, that there are definite 'warning signals' tend-
ing to point to the fact that a posting is about to occur. You
know you are about to be posted when:

— you've just placed an order for 500 address labels
— you've been offered a promotion
— you've finally assembled a list of reliable child caregivers
   who live within walking distance of your house

— your children
  finally admit that
  they like their
  present school
— your children aren't
  pining for their friends
  in the 'old' neighbour-
  hood
— the entire family finally
  knows their postal
  code
— your spouse knows
  both first and last
  names of the
  neighbours on either
  side
— you find that when
  you go shopping, you
  bump into people
  that you actually know

— at least one child is in the middle of complicated and expensive
  orthodontia
— you've finally remodelled and redecorated the entire house
— the asparagus plants, which take three years to mature,
  are ready for harvesting
— your teenage daughter has found that special boyfriend,
  the one she knows she will be absolutely unable to
  live without.

Have I forgotten anything? Do any of these situations sound
familiar to you? It could be that you are also on the move.
Perhaps, as you are preparing to leave, you are asking yourself: "Is there life after Victoria?" (Or substitute other place.)
Here are some personal reflections which may answer that
question.

Four years ago, we arrived in Victoria: two adults, two
kids, two cats; having lived no farther west than Toronto I was
assured that I could be certain of at least two things regarding
our new place of residence. I was told that I would find British

Columbia a beautiful place—and I do. The second point was
the assurance that the weather would be great. I've not much
disagreement on that one either, but I must admit that I've
never really adjusted to the fall in a rain forest.

Being a Maritimer, I was warned in advance, by some
covert east-coast intelligentsia, that westerners simply weren't
as friendly as those dear people on the other side of this
country.

My own initial impressions seemed to confirm this. After
moving into our new house, I used to say to myself: "I wonder
what day a neighbour will come over to say hello?" Then I
started to wonder what week this would happen. Later I'd
wonder what month this might occur. I considered selling
tickets (like the hockey pools) having people guess the date of
the great event! Alas, I didn't know enough people to make
the scheme profitable. Another vexing dilemma for me was
garbage and related topics. Just when we'd deduce that collection day was Tuesday, the next Tuesday the truck would not
appear. Then when we figured out that it was picked up every
second Tuesday, they changed it to Wednesday. What did all
this mean? And another thing, what was all that smoke and
acrid smell in the air on certain days? If only a neighbour
would enlighten me.

Now it is four years later, and I'm happy to say that the
neighbourhood is great and the neighbours are simply the best.
I've learned the intricacies of the waste disposal schedule. I'm
a booster of the one green bag per week rule. I have to admit,
however, that backyard burning is a west-coast tradition that I
did not then and do not now have any interest in making my
own.

The couple who have just purchased our house have
phoned to ask if they can come by and find out some more
about how the house operates. Those things won't take very
long to explain, but there are other things that I'd like to tell
them.

I want to tell them that the best place to do the marketing
is at a small family-owned grocery store. Sam, the owner, and
the rest of the family will take the time to get to know them.

I want to prepare them for the fact that sundry cats and

dogs will occasionally appear at the back door in search of a treat.

I'd like to advise them to keep on hand some tacky possessions for the neighbourhood Christmas party where we recycle our crazy cast-offs.

I'll tell them that on any agreeable Sunday afternoon they may be commandeered for the neighbourhood croquet game on one of our wonderful neighbour's lawns.

After all this I can still say that we are looking forward to our next posting in Halifax. As a family, we'll have the chance to cross the country, visiting friends and relatives scattered along the way. When we arrive, there'll be another comfortable home in yet another great neighbourhood. There'll be a lake for swimming and boating just a five minute walk away. Great beaches, weather permitting, are but a ten minute drive. An assortment of relatives, including grandparents, will now be within easy reach.

And so I think the answer [to the question "Is there life after Victoria?"] is a positive one. I've always left a posting with a heavy heart. I've always looked forward to the next move. For those of us experiencing the military lifestyle, I think it means that I'm normal. The good news is that every new posting has plenty of positives. It's just a matter of time before you find them.

Inspired by Connie's list of indications that a move is in the wind, here are some more 'you know you're posted when'—see just how many relate to you!

You've just bought a house.

Your husband gets promoted.

You've made good friends that you really feel comfortable with.

You can finally find your way around the nearest town/city.

Your flower garden is finally 'picture perfect' after years of loving labour.

Your husband uses 'that tone' to tell you he has a surprise for you.

You just bought that 'once in a lifetime' boat (now you are going to move inland).

You just start to feel like you are sprouting little roots.

CE has *finally* made all those repairs to your PMQ, and you can live without stepping over another worker.

You've finally managed to buy curtains that fit all the windows, and splurged on a wall-to-wall carpet for the living room of your PMQ.

You just got the yard fenced in.

You just purchased that 'second car' after months of 'should I or shouldn't I.'

You've just paid for next year's registration for junior's hockey and missy's ballet lessons.

You're eight months pregnant.

Hubby calls during his six-month UN tour and says "guess what!"

You finally gave in to the kids' pleadings and bought a dog.

You really start to appreciate your surroundings and have become interested in learning as much as you can about the local area.

You're right in the middle of furthering your education at night school.

Your finances are all in order and you've just purchased that much-needed new car (now you have to give up your job and move to a higher rent area).

You broke your leg and will be in a cast for 6-8 weeks.

You just bought a freezer full of beef.

The kids have just completed decorating their own 'space' to suit their tastes and have declared, "Mom, I really like it here now."

The kids have finally established themselves with a good circle of friends and are no longer whining, "I have no one to play with!"

You start to think that maybe, just maybe, the career manager will 'forget' about hubby and leave him here forever.

The thought starts creeping into your subconscious that you've had your fill of moving.

You've finally learned your job well, and feel comfortable and competent in what you are doing.

You've just ordered $50 worth of tulip bulbs for fall planting.

Your husband just finished building that storage shed to house the kids' bikes, lawn mower, etc.

You just moved to a single PMQ after waiting and waiting.

You've finally been able to plan that one special holiday—without the kids.

You're scheduled for surgery.

The career manager has just told hubby that you'll be staying put for another year.

You've finally established a regular clientele for your part-time home business.

You've only one more year to go before retirement.

Your kids are well established in their final years of schooling.

You've just accepted 101 orders for that special craft item that you make that is selling so well.

You've reached the stage where you are confident in the doctor you have chosen—that he really understands your problems.

You've gone through 20 babysitters looking for the 'right one' and have finally found her.

You've joined the base community council to help your fellow neighbours . . .

And now for more insight into this adventurous lifestyle, here is what some of the wives have to say about moving:

Friends Forever: A Moving Experience
by Marcella Kampman

Ten years ago, when my husband was a brand new 2Lt, we were assigned our first posting to the Royal Canadian Dragoons in Lahr, West Germany. Excitedly he told me that he was off to Europe the week after graduation and that I was to follow two weeks later. What he failed to tell me at that time was that I would be handling the move entirely on my own, as he would be going immediately out into the field for Fall EX when he got there.

Somehow, three weeks later with an eight-month-old baby in my arms, I arrived at the Lahr Airfield. It was just after noon and we hadn't eaten since the supper served us on the plane the night before.

My first impression of Lahr was green. Everything was green, the surrounding fields, the buildings, even the furniture!

As I stood there slightly bewildered, with a starving baby in my arms and surrounded by suitcases, a smart, young captain marched up to me. He was the rear party. He handed me a letter from my husband (who was out in the field and scheduled to remain there for four more weeks), then he took me to get a picture ID made in an adjoining room, after which he handed me a key with an address attached to it. It was the key for my new home 2-2-9; the numbers were totally incomprehensible to me. This up and coming officer then told me if there was anything I wanted to give him a call—then proceeded to drive off on his motorcycle!

As I stood there at a complete loss, a wonderful woman approached me with a bouquet of flowers in her hand. She was the wife of my husband's Squadron Commander and she just wanted to welcome me to Germany. Blank astonishment turned to horror on her face at the dawning realization that I was left stranded at the airport, with a now starving infant, and no one to pick me up or look after me. As for my own features, they were too tired to register anything. My reaction to the word "Sponsor" was the same as to the strange code in which my address was written. What does it mean? I learned later that we were never assigned this wonderful "Sponsor" person who was supposed to greet, guide and in every way smooth out the way for our move.

Bonnie bundled us up in her car, and being new to Lahr herself, took us on a long exploration to find the building which belonged to the strangely coded numbers. Once finally in the apartment, we discovered that nothing had been looked after or arranged; there was no baby furniture, no bedding or dishes and no food. Poor Bonnie was nearly in despair but seeing how tired and hungry we were, she quickly took charge.

She brought us over to a neighbour and while Kathy cared for us and fed us, Bonnie single-handedly organized the arrival of a playpen and other amenities. She had the rear party hopping in no time.

Later that afternoon, settled in my own apartment, the traditional Lahr flu hit me full force. I staggered next door and thrust my baby into Kathy's arms before making a beeline for her bathroom. When I weakly made my reappearance, she informed me that she had called another wife who was willing to stay with me for the evening so that I wouldn't be alone. Heather arrived promptly and proceeded to take excellent care of us.

In short order I had met several of the officers' wives. Of course these introductions were not under the most ideal of situations, and yet, I believe strongly that it was the crisis of the moment and the outstanding support I received that first day that led to my ongoing and continuing friendships with these wonderfully caring women. Friendships which might have taken longer to blossom in a more 'ideal' setting.

While we were together in Germany these ladies became more than my friends, they were my mentors as well as wonderful role models.

It is now ten years later and the years have sent us on our separate ways. Often the only time we hear from each other is at Christmas. This past December my husband was suddenly sent to Somalia with his entire squadron. Two of the first calls I received for moral support and encouragement were from Bonnie and Kathy. Both now live in different cities from me, yet when they learned of this peacemaking operation, they didn't hesitate a moment to call. Not only to chat (and offer advice) but also to let me know that they are out there and that they are living through this with me as well. And that after all these years, they are still my friends.

Western Girl Comes East
by Carol Asbury

My first glimpse of Nova Scotia was at 3:00 a.m. December 14, 1991. My life has forever changed. Being from the Prairies,

Winnipeg to be exact, I recognize that gravity kicks in when driving the streets of Halifax. My car has never worked so hard. You can hear it gasping for breath on each and every hill. I have also experienced a ferry ride: "Please pay one token to pass the gate, then follow several people and get on a boat about to tackle waves, and bring you safely to Halifax." It took me several rides to get my sea legs and a calm stomach. No traffic jams, or bad tempered drivers, just white capped waves, seagulls the size of basketballs, and the aromatic smell of fresh fish. Token number two comes into play when you cross one of the monsters called bridges. My heart skipped several beats when I first laid eyes on them. What holds them up? Will I make it across? Will the wind blow me over the edge? It's not often in Manitoba that our feet are that high off the ground.

All kidding aside, I have great respect for military women, be they wives, girlfriends, friends, etc. I came out to Halifax to be with my boyfriend. He's in the Army. I left behind my best friend Pat, my parents, my brothers and my nephews. All these people have a very special part in my life. They all have a little piece of my heart. There are many days I felt so home-sick, I just cried until there were no tears left. It almost feels like your heart is breaking. It takes courage to be a military wife, lots of love, patience, a fearless heart, and lots of energy.

These past few months have been an experience, but as they say, "growth can be painful" and you grow stronger from pain. I have learned to depend on myself, and I'm learning new things about myself every day. It's my determination that gets me through all the rough moments, nothing else. I have gotten involved with the church, I work part time, and I'm vol-unteering some time at the Military Family Resource Centre. I also have applied to become a Big Sister, which will allow me to share some of my love and caring with a little girl who needs it, and at the same time it will help me grow.

So as you can see, being involved makes your move to a new area much easier.

Time to Take the Quantum Leap
by Crystal G. Mann

Well, it's that time of the year again! No not Spring fever, POSTING SEASON!!! As this next posting season approaches, I find myself torn between wanting to stay put and wanting to go off on a new adventure. For those fortunate not to have to move (I guess that depends on whether you like where you are) I congratulate as well as envy you. For those of you who will soon be on your way, I am both ecstatic and sympathetic for what you are about to go through.

My father was in the Forces, and during my childhood I moved several times. I was under five for the first two and eleven the third time. That one was the big move of my childhood and I was devastated. I felt that my whole world was just turned upside down. I felt so lost in a strange place. I missed my friends, all the amenities—where was I going to "hang out" and with whom? I wasn't even sure who I was anymore.

Since getting married seven years ago, my military husband has been posted five times (wait for it), and during this time I have personally and physically packed up and moved 7 times (honestly!!!). Each time I had to go through a similar process. Oh, where am I? When is this? What am I this time? Wife, mother, housewife, student, working woman, SUPER WOMAN or all of the above??? The hardest questions being, who am I this time? I'm a survivor? Just barely getting by? Or a thriver? I'm feeling so good about myself and so sure of things I can't lose because I'm a winner!

Well, if any of you have ever seen the series "Quantum Leap," you might understand what it feels like to be 'gypsy' type people. The main character is guided by a Hologram (guardian angel) while he jumps in and out of peoples' bodies and lives. One minute he is a college football player and the next he's a mother with children; he never knows who he'll be next or what time warp he'll be in.

The correlation between the show and my life came one night as I was driving home on the highway. It was a little after midnight and I was pretty tired. All of a sudden I thought

I was back at the last place we lived (three provinces away); then it occurred to me that I didn't know where I was. OH MY GOSH! WHERE AM I? Where do I live? Then it clicked in, and was I relieved. As in the show, I feel like one minute I'm on my way to the office, and the next I'm in this strange kitchen making lunch for my children. Time warp, twilight zone, call it what you will, it sure is exhausting getting used to this way of life (is that what you call this?). This was not the first time this happened to me. Do you know how many times I've been asked for my address or phone number and I either gave my previous one or forgot altogether. Sometimes I just mix them all up; new address, old province, postal code before that one. Disassociated or what! I've gone through so many people, places and things that I'm often questioning my own experiences. "Excuse me, do I know you from somewhere before or did we just meet?" I'm surprised I can remember my name, let alone new information like phone numbers, addresses, license plate numbers, etc.

The part I find most exciting about moving around so much, is that you don't have to get divorced to be married to different men. One posting he's a student, one a paper pusher, another a 'frenchman' yet another a sailor. With each new job my husband seems to take on different behaviour patterns. Different interests, ways of expressing himself, even the way he dresses and speaks, and strangely enough, different habits (some not worth mentioning). All these changes brought on by the "QUANTUM LEAP."

On the Road Again
by Carol Nethercott

The news you have either been awaiting or dreading has finally come, usually via your spouse and worded something like— "Honey, we're being posted." My reaction to this has either been exhiliaration or dismay, depending upon where we have been posted.

Looking back over the past 28 years, there is no doubt in

my mind the very first move was definitely the easiest. Back in the late sixties we had one 15-month-old son, a few sticks of furniture and a car. Piece of cake!! Wrong! The train trip across Canada in mid-December was anything but. The train was shunted off to a side track near Winnipeg to await rail clearing for nearly eight hours, during which time the pipes froze so we had neither running water nor flushing toilets or hot food. Have you ever been sequestered in a tiny roomette with a baby, tons of clean and not so clean diapers, all of us fully dressed in coats and boots to keep warm and nothing to do? The other joy was mealtime when we slogged our way through connecting cars (knee deep in snow) to the dining car only to have the baby howl with pain each time he was placed on the baby seat provided by CN. It was stored in an unheated cupboard when not in use, so naturally it froze between meals. I'm sure the dining car staff really looked forward to our visit three times a day.

Subsequent moves brought their own ups and downs. Two more sons, a dog, a cat, a house, lots more furniture, two cars—a moving company's nightmare! Then it was necessary to convince the kids that their next school was going to be just great, they would meet lots of new and interesting friends and join wonderful new groups. Easier said than done!! First there was instant refusal on their part to move, then, gradually, questions were asked about the new area we were moving to and finally a general excitement about the actual move—aided in part by the fact that all kids love hotels, eating out and swimming pools!

As the children matured into young adults, posting took on a whole new spectre. One or more of these fine young adults, whom we have nurtured to be independent, responsible and worldly, would demonstrate these same qualities by deciding that they have had enough moves and want to either stay in their current university or attend one thousands of miles from where you have been posted. That's when you suddenly realize the years pass all too quickly and now the family unit is breaking up. Not only that, you flinch at how much it is going to cost in real dollars to assist these young people in leaving the nest. We have had three of them do it and believe me, I qualify as an expert in financial management. There is, however, a light at the end of the tunnel.

Reflecting on our life in the military, I can't help but think how very lucky I have been to have had the experiences of travelling across Canada, Europe and the Far East, experiencing different cultures and making new friends in the places we have lived. We have maintained these friendships, both military and civilian, over the years and Christmas seems to be the time that we get caught up with the lives of all these people through their letters, pictures and cards. Some of them we will probably never see again, but that doesn't lessen the personal contact we maintain each year. Moves and postings bring hassles and frustrations. Along with the ones I have touched upon, there are others such as house buying and selling, job changes for yourself and saying goodbye to family and friends—nobody said it was going to be easy! It is simply another step along life's many experiences.

Having raised three fine young men who are making their way in the world, having given them some of our furniture along with their bedroom suites when they left, having had to put our 13-year-old ailing Sheltie to sleep a few months ago, we are down to one car and oh yes, we still have a cat (Sweet Pea) who is 11 years old. We call her our only child now. My husband calls it "downsizing." I think we have one more posting ahead of us, should be a piece of cake, right?

I have moved 11 times in 25 years—six of which were moves we did ourselves. Our first move was from a furnished apartment upstairs to one directly at the bottom of the stairs. It was to set the tone for most of our moves but I didn't know it at the time. Yes, you guessed it, come time to move and my husband was away. I had a few cardboard boxes and two plastic laundry baskets and that's how I moved. I also had an infant to care for. I packed these boxes and laundry baskets, then took my baby downstairs and lugged these boxes down and unpacked them. Then I took my baby upstairs, loaded the boxes again and repeated the procedure until all our belong-

ings were moved. To this day I hate stairs with a passion. It would be different if I had lost a few pounds through all this exercising—that would have been an unexpected bonus—but it just didn't happen . . .

✳   ✳   ✳

We were married for 17 years before my other half hung his first curtain rod—he was just never around long enough to do it. In those days, PMQs didn't come with curtain rods and believe me, I sure had a large collection of them at one point. No two windows were ever the same size!! On our last posting here, we moved into our PMQ on Thursday, and that Saturday my husband was in Valcartier, Quebec on exercise. So I could either wait 5-6 weeks until he came home to hang the curtains—or do it myself.

Advice

For those who are contemplating yet another move, here is some helpful advice from other wives to make the move a little easier.

First, believe nothing that you hear. As well meaning as some people are, and as quick as they are to offer advice, FIND OUT FOR YOURSELF. And that holds true of every aspect of military life. The first thing I was told by a neighbour when she heard that we were coming to Petawawa was that I would hate it here and that there were cockroaches in all the PMQs. If you listen to what other people tell you, you could find yourself just dreading making the move and not enjoying the travelling that goes with it. Everyone looks at things differently. What was negative for your well-meaning neighbour might be positive for you—except the bugs that is . . . I never did find any!

When you find out the location of your next posting, write the tourist bureau at your new location and ask for any pamphlets they have on attractions and points of interest in that general area. If you plan on definite stops en route, then obtain brochures from those travel bureaus as well. Don't wait for an information package from your husband's new unit. Some bases give out really good packages, while others don't, and some give out information that is outdated. I remember sending the boys to BP Lodge one Saturday morning, as the information book I received said there were movies for the kids every Saturday morning and we lived close by. Well, the boys waited and waited and no one showed up—they came home very upset and crying. I later found out they had stopped the movies about two years before.

Keep these tourist brochures for your actual trip. When the kids are getting restless, or seem really sad and apprehensive about the 'unknowns' of their new posting, then haul out one of the brochures and share it with them and talk about it.

Before your trip, buy some small story books, colouring books, diaries, or notebooks depending on the ages of your children. Don't let the kids know you have them until you are actually on your way. Then when they get restless, give them something new to help pass the time and hold their interest for a while.

At stops along the way let the kids send postcards to the friends they have left behind.

This is a great time to play games—again depending on the ages of your children. You have the kids as a captive audience in the car, so go over some very important things they should keep fresh in their minds. But make a game of it. For instance, you could ask them:

What would you do if

1. a stranger offers you candy to go for a ride in his car
2. you were lost
3. there was a fire in the house

and so on. Then talk about the answers they gave you.

Encourage older children to keep a diary of events as you travel to your new home. It will be something to write to their old friends about when they settle down in their new location and also might come in handy as a school project.

Once you get to your destination, let the kids be responsible for unpacking and arranging their own room—when they see their familiar things it will help them settle in. Fear of the unknown is quickly put to rest when kids have favourite blankets, toys and other belongings in their new surroundings.

If your kids are interested in sports, don't hesitate to sign them up even though the season might be halfway through. In the summer particularly, it's a great opportunity for the kids to make some friends before school starts and that is important. Nothing can be more painful than going to a new school when they don't know anyone. If they can make a friend or two beforehand, it really does ease the apprehension.

I have one son that adjusted in a snap to our moves; the other had a very difficult time. When we were leaving one posting and had a new house to sell, Trevor overheard my husband John and me discussing what selling price we would put on the house and our worries about whether it would sell. We were discussing whether to repair all the pin holes in the walls in the boy's bedrooms (from their hockey pennants) and then whether we would have to paint the rooms before we put the house up for sale. He told his brother Chris that they should hammer nail holes in all the walls—that way no one would want to buy our house and then we wouldn't have to move! It was funny, but it showed how desperately he didn't want to make the move. We were then able to talk to him more and ease his fears of moving. We also hid the hammer just in case . . .

As for yourself, the first bit of advice—travel light. Many wives find it easier to re-wash a few clothes than to be saddled with too many. There is less hassle with the kids if they are also limited with the number of clothes they have to choose from. Nothing is worse than being cooped up in a motel for a couple of weeks with two or three kids while Dad is off to work. They soon tire of restaurant food and get restless easily. And it is usually Mom that has the responsibility of trying to keep the kids happy until your new home is available.

A travel routine that worked well for many of us should be given some thought:

— leave around 6 a.m. (kids often fall back to sleep once they are in the car and moving)
—stop for breakfast about 10 a.m.
—stop for lunch around 2 p.m. (you miss the noon rush hour at restaurants then)
—stop for the day around 4-5 p.m. (that way there is time for the kids to have a swim in the pool if one is available or they can watch a bit of TV and generally unwind before a good supper and early bedtime).

I always left a posting with a heavy heart, sad to leave friends and the life we had established there, but excited about this new adventure and what the next posting might have in store for us. But one posting was harder to leave than all the others, and that was Chilliwack, British

Columbia. It was about as far away from our relatives at home as we could get, but we were really happy there. I had the best job I ever had since we were married, and we had a lovely home with lots of fruit trees and a huge garden which we all loved. The boys had many friends their own age all living close by and were really busy with all their sports and activities. But most of all, we lived right in the City of Chilliwack about 10 miles from the base and had made so many good, civilian friends. It was just very difficult to leave it all behind—especially the friends because I felt that chances were that we might never see them again. I knew by then that we always seemed to bump into military friends in our travels and that was always such a great part of this lifestyle.

As we were preparing to leave the area, I didn't even want to look at our home for 'one last time' and I started crying. My husband clocked me—said I cried for 30 miles!! It was such a sad day. But our friends had given us a terrific send-off with a neighbourhood party the night before we left. Our vehicle was not left out of the celebrations either. When we left the neighbour's house to return to the motel, there was our truck in the rain, completely covered with toilet paper inside and out— not to mention the flour on all the windows. It seems that it was pay-back time for some of the Halloween pranks we had played over our years there. The funny part of the whole incident was that our boys had seen the prank done on our vehicle earlier in the evening and retaliated with the car of the neighbour who was hosting the party thinking they were responsible (they weren't . . .). Poor thing, she got up late for work as a teacher the next morning and found her car completely entwined in toilet paper! We had many laughs on reminiscing as we drove away, but it just made the move that much sadder.

Movers

Many horror stories have surfaced where precious family items have been 'lost,' broken, or damaged. Some have been irreplaceable items. Moving for many military families can become a nightmare.

Most of the wives surveyed felt the movers were definitely not careful enough with their belongings. While safeguards seem to be in place to allow complaining about an unsatisfactory move, nothing can compensate for irreplacable items. Those with sentimental value just cannot be measured in dollars and cents! Years ago 30 cents per pound was all the moving company was liable for in compensating individuals for damage. Therefore, a bunch of fishing rods (one handmade) held together by elastic bands and stood up in a corner behind a door only amounted to a couple of dollars in compensation when the tips of the rods rested in the crack of an open door which a mover promptly shut! Subsequent settlement of a claim through military insurance did not cover the cost of the replacement with new rods. However, today military families only have to deal with one agency when negotiating to settle a moving claim and I understand this system seems to work much better.

On one move from British Columbia to Ontario the mover's estimate of damage to our belongings totaled over $3,000 (my estimate was higher). With my husband away much of that year, I had to deal with the insurance adjuster. It took one week short of a year to get compensation and many, many upsetting phone conversations with the adjuster. He literally did his best to wear me down. The more money he could save on this payout, the better it looked for him and *not once* did he set foot in our home to examine any of the items we reported damaged or destroyed (including a beautiful 6-foot wooden stereo and cabinet from Germany which was irreplaceable).

In general, the wives feel that if the mover's responsibility for damages was substantially higher than the current $1.00 per hundredweight liability, they would take greater care in the handling of our belongings.

It is upsetting to work hard for your possessions only to have them ruined or 'lost' by uncaring movers. On the other hand, we have had some movers who were very thoughtful and helpful and who did many extras they were not obliged to do, like taking my large boxes of plants from Ontario to British Columbia (and back again four years later) and even watering them along the way.

Still, with the thousands of military moves done yearly and the excellent money paid out to the movers, we deserve better treatment than we are getting.

In our last move six years ago DND paid the movers $480 for unpacking our belongings and yet we did all the unpacking ourselves! The cost is pre-determined based on the total weight of your move. Granted, if you unpack yourself, the moving company is then not liable for any damage you uncover but, from my experience, I suspect most movers don't mention to their superiors that they did not actually do the unpacking and most military families do not mention that they did the unpacking.

The fact is, many wives prefer to unpack slowly once they have more time to decide just where everything is to go. Therefore, the movers are being paid for nothing! There has to be a better system. In times of financial restraints, perhaps DND could review and revamp the current setup of payouts to movers.

Chapter 10

The Blue Bonnet

Like the Blue Beret so proudly worn by members of the Canadian Armed Forces when serving on UN tours, there is an invisible 'blue bonnet' worn by the wives of these servicemen. Proud of their husbands' involvement, apprehensive about their safety and completely responsible for home and family and all that it entails, these women take on the dual role of mother and father for six months at a time and others for a year or more.

Throughout this section you will read poems and articles written by the women closest to the servicemen. Their message comes straight from the heart.

Insurance

My life, as I know it today, would cease to exist should my husband die. I am here because of him; my friends are his buddies' wives, my job is gone because I left it behind, my house is a PMQ. My life is his life.

A few serious words to both husbands and wives are in order here before we get further into this chapter. What would you do if tomorrow your life changed forever because of the death or disability of your wife or husband, or one of your children? Are you prepared financially? Do you have adequate insurance? Human nature being what it is, we all tend to think that nothing is ever going to happen to us—upsetting things only happen to other people. No one likes to talk about 'those things.' When you're young, you tend to think, 'I'll live until I'm old, there is plenty of time to think about 'those things' tomorrow!' When we talk about UN taskings, certainly the increased danger the men face is uppermost in our minds. But are we realizing that anything could happen to any one of us at any time—regardless of where we are? Are you prepared for that?

Insurance is an 'intangible.' You keep paying for it but you see nothing for your investment—so why bother? Why? Because tomorrow you could be without a husband or without a wife. How will you and your children manage then? Take insurance seriously and make sure that you are all properly covered, whether it's through your own personal insurance or through the military plan (SISIP). It is not enough to just have coverage on your husband. What if the wife dies? Who is going to look after the children? How are you going to afford help? Regardless of how you are struggling as a young couple starting out, remember that the younger you are, the cheaper the rates. Do without those fancy coffee tables for now and put that money into a sound insurance plan. The younger you are, the cheaper the rates. Please don't be one of those who says, "If only I had known . . ." Take good care of yourselves.

✻   ✻   ✻

Cyprus
Separation (at Its Best)

The time is fast approaching,
The men are all in line.
The plane is on the runway,
To be gone for six months time.

Now's the time to be inventive,
To help the time go by.
We work all day and into night,
Thinking of that super special guy.

With holidays coming upon us,
And birthdays and anniversaries too.
We'll just sit back, be patient,
Trying not to sing the blues.

Family, friends, they come around,
To see if we're in need.
Whether it's to simply talk,
Or just for a good night's feed.

Children, they're the hardest,
Their daddies had to go.
To try to understand this,
Their response is simply no.

Within this time allotted,
The mothers do their best.
To answer all the questions,
They're put to the test.

Phone calls are an added bonus.
They help to make us smile.
Just to hear his voice say hi,
Brings you nearer to those miles.

We love our spouses dearly,
And with them all the way.
On this we praise them highly,
And wait for our reunion day.

Hugs and kisses will follow,
We're ecstatic as can be.
We rush them to the homefront,
And throw away the key.

—Linda Gardiner
For her husband Jim (lst Battalion, The Royal
Canadian Regiment) while he served in Cyprus.

✳   ✳   ✳

Cyprus, Egypt and Alert, N.W.T. were once the 'normal' six-month postings. While the danger to servicemen was perhaps not as great in the last few years as it has been for the subsequent UN taskings to Iran/Iraq, Somalia, Croatia or the former Yugoslavia, these postings still represented a long period of time for husbands to be away.

My husband did three UN tours—7 1/2 months in Egypt and
two 6-month tours in Cyprus. If I had to consult with him
before any decisions were made, they just wouldn't get made!
And you can't live like that for such long periods of time. As a

matter of fact, he was in Cyprus when my son was born. He was our third child and I told the doctor I wanted my tubes tied. He wasn't going to do it because my husband wasn't there. That really made me mad. It's my body . . . Anyway, I really think the only reason he did do it was because we had two daughters and then a son and the doctor was of the old school. You know, every father wants a son. I think if my third child had been a girl, he would have refused to do it.

❋   ❋   ❋

From a newlywed:

When he was returning from Cyprus, I was so excited when I went to meet him. Here were all these guys and I kept looking for him through the crowd and then, there he was. I've never felt such strong emotions in my life!

❋   ❋   ❋

While my husband was in Cyprus, I was playing ball one day with our five kids. One of my sons got behind me where I didn't see him and I accidentally hit him on the head with the bat. I had to take him to the hospital but first I had to get someone to look after the other four kids. No one had a car at home to take me to the hospital and since I didn't drive I had to scrape some money together to take a taxi. It was money that I really couldn't spare and the hospital was quite a few miles away in Barrie.

We had to wait a couple of days for the test results and thank heavens all was OK, but by then I was a nervous wreck! It didn't help that my husband had just sent me a picture from Cyprus of him and some friends sitting around having a drink with the sun and sand in the background. The whole situation made me so mad. I wrote my husband and told him it was all his fault for being away and if he had been home none of this would have happened! Right after I mailed the letter I felt guilty. It really wasn't his fault his job took him away from us.

❋   ❋   ❋

During my husband's 36 years' service he was away five times on six-month postings. On one of those tours, he was only back-up to go. A friend of ours who was in the same trade, the same rank, was scheduled to go. He and his wife had no children—we had five. She just didn't want her husband to go and said she'd have a 'nervous breakdown' if he went away. Sure enough, two weeks before he was due to leave she had her 'breakdown' and my husband had to go in his place. It just wasn't fair. By the time my youngest child was 24 months old her father had been away on exercises, courses and UN tour for 22 of those months! She didn't know who this man was and wouldn't go near him. It took a good three weeks before she would accept him.

I don't think it's fair that one man should have to serve so many six-month tours in his career. Surely there are enough men in the Army that this should not happen. It seems if you are a 'problem' or 'make waves' you get out of doing these things but if you keep a low profile and just do your job, you get the shaft!

One of the difficult things I had to deal with was when we moved to Calgary when I was pregnant. A large portion of the unit was in Cyprus, so my husband had called ahead of time to see if he would be required to go to Cyprus. If so, he was going to leave us where we were since we had friends handy to help while he was gone. He was told that he would not be required in Cyprus, so off we went to Calgary. Three days after we arrived he was on his way to Cyprus. I didn't know the city and I was huge with my pregnancy (my son weighed 11 lbs. 10 ozs.) and it was difficult for me to drive. The house needed fixing up. Being new to the base, I didn't want to make waves, but felt so depressed with our situation. It was hard to deal with all this and with the fact that my husband would not be there when I had the baby. No matter what we were facing I always tried very hard not to cry, but this was one time that I just couldn't hold the tears back.

Cyprus Letters

by Major Bill Leavey

Six long months of peacekeeping duty on Aphrodite's Isle were almost over. The troops were restless. As repatriation dates approached, the passionate detail of letters from home intensified. One spirited, recently married, young soldier was particularly anxious to return. In a final letter, he instructed his young bride to "Have a mattress in the back of the van at the airport." Her equally spirited reply was classic: "Make sure you're the first one off the plane!"

When my husband was in Cyprus, I had a very difficult birth. The hospital did not have my blood type on file and my brother-in-law ended up being the donor for my blood transfusion. My Mom was with me at the hospital at first, but then she went home to tend to the children. The hospital did not notify her as they were supposed to do when my son was born. As a result, when my husband called all Mom told him was that I had been admitted to the hospital—but no news yet! My Mom phoned the hospital later that day and they casually told her all was OK. She had to pry out of them that I had had difficulties and she was very upset. A message was sent to my husband notifying him that he had a son, but it took five days before he received that message. Thank heavens he called again that day and found then that his son was born. Thank heavens for phones, but they are awful hard on the pocketbook at times.

Tribute to UN Forces

We see you on T.V.
Trying to do your job,
Amongst the flying bullets
We see women and children sob.

Your job is an important one
Even if you question it,
For you're a UN soldier
It's your job to do your best.
You wear a Blue Beret
That has been around through much,
He did his time in Cyprus
And at times life got pretty rough.

He wore the badge with so much pride
And knew what it stood for.
He was proud to be a Canadian
And part of the United Nations Corps.

So to each and every comrade
Wear that Hat with pride,
Because your job's a vital one
You're keeping a country alive.

—Barbara Rodler
Written in loving memory of her brother, Cpl Quinn H.
Smith, lst Battalion, The Royal Canadian Regiment,
who died on leave July l9, l992 as a result of a
motor vehicle accident in Nova Scotia.

Namibia
An Open Letter to My Husband in Namibia

Another day is here now—only 62 to go!
At least that's what the news is—
It's been changed so much you know.

I was so happy for you, that day we said goodbye;
"I'll be back before you know it," you said,
And I tried hard not to cry.

But there are days I wonder to myself—
Will we really make it through?

I didn't think it would be this hard
To be so far away from you.

You've been away a lot before
On RVs and on courses,
And yes, I knew when I married you
that you were in the Forces.

But this time it seems different,
No matter how I feel
Africa's a place in books—
it's not a place that's real.

I really miss you badly and until
that ole' plane lands,
I'll pray for you each day, dear,
and place you in God's hands.

Your Loving Wife

—Julie A. Doherty
Written for her husband Sergeant
Steve Doherty, 2nd Service Battalion

Namibia was one of the first departures from the regular taskings, and some wives were concerned about whether there would be an abundance of alcohol and prostitutes where their husbands were going. A serviceman who has been there responded to these concerns: "Those same temptations are wherever you are—they are here and they are there. It really depends on your husband's inclinations. So don't worry any more about those things when he is away than you would when he is home. If he is inclined that way he will find an opportunity!"

Good communication and trust are essential in military marriages. One wife summed it up well when she said, "You have to work hard in any marriage but in a military marriage you have to work 10 times as hard." The men might have more opportunities to be unfaithful as they are constantly away for long periods of time but, as one respondent says, "Neither of you can spend your days wondering if you are each being faithful—because if you do, the mistrust will eventually destroy your marriage. You just have to have good communication so you can keep in tune with each other's concerns and needs and you just have to trust each other when you are alone."

Iran/Iraq

As the war in the Persian Gulf unfolded and Canadian Forces were sent from Petawawa, there was a great deal of media coverage. One of the questions most commonly asked of military wives by interviewers was: "How do you feel about your husband going to the Gulf?" Well, if you stop and think about it, this question is rather pointless. How do you think they felt? No one was overjoyed, that's for sure. As time progressed and we saw our troops being sent to Somalia, the former Yugoslavia and Croatia, this type of question was still being asked and remained just as pointless.

Seeing a husband off for an indefinite period of time is nothing new for military wives. What was new with these taskings was the increased danger to their husbands and of course, with that, the increased worry at home.

I watched one TV interviewer who was talking with a military wife of many years. The interviewer seemed to be doing her best to portray the doom and gloom of the situation. I was so pleased to see the military wife not get caught up in this attempt at sensationalizing. She remained calm and stated several times, "We are doing OK, we will carry on!" Good for her! For a while I felt that some of the media were deliberately attempting to just get as sensational a story as they could—the more upset the lady appeared, the bettter the interview! But after I observed several stories and interviews, I realized *they just do not understand what we are all about!* The doom and gloom is what the interviewers would be feeling in the same situation and not necessarily what they are trying to portray as fact.

To most civilians, seeing your husband depart for six months at a time might be unthinkable—for military wives it's par for the course. Yes, these recent tours were very different, and yes, there were many worries and uncertainties as to the dangers that lay ahead. But no, military wives do not turn to Jello because their husbands are gone.

Military wives do go through many emotions when their husbands are gone, trying to cope with a magnitude of problems, with the agony of trying to make all the 'right' decisions by themselves, and dealing with children who are feeling the absence of their father. But in the midst of all these emotions, a sense of humour can emerge at the least expected times. "I was in the hospital in labour for our son when my husband's Sergeant called him at the hospital. He told him to tell me that he was going to the Gulf and like a good soldier my husband told me! Needless to say, it didn't help ease my labour pains . . ."

✱   ✱   ✱

For others, a UN tasking generates not only a change in the service member, but a maturing of the family as a whole:

I have seen a definite change in my husband since he came home from the Gulf. There is now an awareness about him and he talks more intently. This was one positive outcome of this particular separation—you stop drifting from day to day.

My son who is 12 is starting to understand. When his Dad went to the Persian Gulf it was a very scary time for all of us, and of course he had to deal with anger. He and his father were becoming very close, at a time when it's important for children to have that 'closeness' and then his father was taken away from him. This situation was real—it was no longer fun and games or 'pretending'—the real danger was definitely there.

Plans were made for my child and me to go home for Christmas (Ottawa to Winnipeg). You know how hard it is to make reservations at Christmas time. My husband might be home—he didn't know for sure. If he came home, and I had already gone to Winnipeg, the military couldn't give any assurance they would bring him to me. If I stayed here in Petawawa and my husband didn't get home then I would be alone for Christmas. If I went to Winnipeg and he did get home, he might not be able to join us and then he would be alone for the holidays. We just couldn't win!

I told my husband that if they tried to take him away somewhere else when he got back from Iran/Iraq I would kidnap him and take him somewhere where they could never find him.

My husband was in the Persian Gulf for four months; we were living in Germany at the time. When he came back, we had to make the move to Petawawa. Most of our furniture was destroyed in the move. Here it is nine months later, we still are not settled with the insurance and he has been in RV 92 for three months. It has definitely been a trying time for the children and me, and for my husband too!

Western Sahara

When the Airborne were preparing to go to the Western Sahara, I really worried about them going to battle without the proper equipment. As a mechanic, my husband knows the condition of some of their equipment—it's old and way past its prime. You can paint a vehicle, spruce it up and polish the tires, but if it doesn't respond when you turn the key in the ignition, what good is it to you?

A friend of mine had planned a December wedding but her fiance was scheduled to go to Africa with the Airborne Regiment. Her wedding plans had to be changed and everything cancelled. As with most deployments of this type, the day-by-day uncertainty of not knowing just 'when' the men were going to leave created more stress. As it happened, this deployment was ultimately cancelled—but too late to reschedule the wedding. So the couple ended up getting married in June and the bride wore her winter wedding dress in the heat of the summer!

Somalia
Deployment

*How will you help the people in despair—
by bringing a little love over there.*

For love is the greatest legacy you will provide,
deliver it freely, it is something you must not hide.

Never doubt not having enough love to give—
because of you, others will live.

Your courage will never falter,
for with your love—their world you alter.

So hold your head high, showing dignity, mercy and grace,
because you are making their country a safer place.

Listen with your heart as well as your ears,
for with compassion, not judgement, will you dry their tears.

Please remember as you help to end their sadness and cloud,
because of you, we are a country proud!

—Michelle Posthumus
This valentine poem was dedicated to her husband
Corporal Steve Posthumus, lst Battalion, The Royal
Canadian Regiment, and all the other brave soldiers in
Somalia who were helping to make a difference.

For those whose husbands were off to Somalia, fears for their safety were paramount, but other fears also surfaced. Here are some of the initial reactions to news of deployment:

Scared! What would happen to the boys (3 1/2, 1 yr, 3 mos)
and me? What would it do to our marriage? I would miss him
too much!

Glad to see he's helping others and putting training to use but
hated to see him go, naturally.

Very upset that I was left with the unusual responsibility of
supervising construction of a house and moving alone.

Relief after the 'yes we are, no we aren't'!

Overwhelming loneliness.

First minute—SHOCK! He was just back from a five-month course, but it's part of his work.

One wife's comments stood out:
What's another six months when we've already been apart almost a year. I hope it won't be too dangerous.

She went on to answer the question 'How did she prepare the children (2 and 4 1/2) for Daddy's leaving' by saying:
They hadn't seen him more than 28 days in a year so they can't miss what they've never had—a full-time Dad!

The children (10 and 12) are way too sad, way too often.

Worried about having an emergency I can't handle.

He's missing the baby's first year.

Mostly wondering what it will be like getting to know each other again.

Eight Weeks Down

Eight weeks down, I dare not count the ones left to go. Eight weeks of gazing at pictures, recalling memories, and trying to explain to a child, not yet two years old, where daddy is, and that daddy is doing something wonderful for some very unfortunate people who live on the other side of the world.

Somehow, through the tears and screams, there is a bright, shining, and warm light, that pierces through the darkness of missing someone so much. A truth that is comforting beyond what we can conceive. A truth which explains to us that there is good reason for all events which tumble across our life's path, whether they are good or seem bad.

So during this separation, let us learn and grow stronger. Let us grow in the wisdom of what is truth. Let us be strong

*for those who are so fragile. May we grow in strength, so that
when we are reunited with our loved one, we can show our
love more than we ever have, and we can accept those things
which we may never be able to change, and we can support
our loved one in a career which we do not fully understand.
Let us benefit from this separation so we can examine ourselves and perhaps change those things which our spouse
might find undesirable. Yes, this time can be used in so many
wonderful ways.*

*Let us utilize these desperate times in ways which will help
us grow closer to our loved one and let us absorb those quiet
moments and refresh our spirits so that when our loved one
returns home, we will be there not only in body, but more
importantly, in clean spirit, with no resentment, but in ultimate
love and support.*

—Delia Speed
A loving and supportive wife to her husband,
Corporal Daniel K. Speed, Canadian Airborne Regiment.

*Our daughter is only three years old—too young to under-
stand what is going on. All she knows is that her Dad is not
here. He has a different relationship with the kids than I do.
Because he's away so much he tries to have quality time with
the children. He's 'God' and I'm a cross between Oscar the
Grouch and the Wicked Witch!*

Of great importance to many families was the need to explain to the
children that this time Daddy's departure was different. Many stressed
that Daddy was going to help feed the starving children. One 4 1/2 year
old immediately went to the cupboard and took out her box of Ritz
crackers and gave them to her Daddy to help feed the children.

*I told the oldest (3 1/2) that Daddy had to go away to the place
on TV to work to help the sick boys and girls.*

*Told them (5 yrs, 7 months) as much as possible without
making too much of it.*

Sat them (10 and 12) down and told them I had bad news, gave them the bad news, hugged and cried together. All that three weeks before Christmas!

Talked about where, why and when he was leaving and tried to be very honest.

We showed them (6 and 2) on the map where he was going and why.

We didn't do anything special, to the children (10, 7, 5), Daddy was simply leaving and would be back around the end of the school year.

Daddy is always gone only the location changes. What's new?

She was only two, my husband told her to take good care of Mommy and gave her a photo of himself to kiss good night and good morning.

We told them (6 and 9) that he had to go to do important work, that he would be gone a long time but that they would be fine here.

Media

Wives whose husbands were in Somalia and the former Yugoslavia expressed similar thoughts when asked how they felt about media reports on the troubled areas their husbands were in.

They should remember that these men have families and to stop sensationalizing news reports.

Scared—especially when they say a general comment like "Two Canadians Hurt" or "One Dead"—you think, which one?

It sounds like my husband has spent 5 1/2 months away from home and accomplished nothing!

Greatly sensationalized and only available when there's something 'gory' happening!

Can you really believe what the media is telling us?

In general, the women felt there was not enough Canadian coverage but were grateful for any information they could get: "I'm happy with any news, even the slightest bit of information that helps me to understand." On the media issue, the ladies were divided—some watched every single TV report and read all the newspaper articles, while others chose to rely only on information from their husbands and from his unit/rear party.

Canadian Airborne Regiment

During this tour the media presented allegations of improper conduct by members of the Airborne Regiment in Somalia. As a result, Airborne wives and families wearing their distinctive Airborne T-shirts were sometimes harrassed by civilians in nearby Pembroke. Although the actions of only a few, it was enough to really upset the wives who were already dealing with a whole range of emotions new to them all—certainly more than they should be expected to have to deal with. This was rather the last straw. Condemnation of the civilians' actions immediately followed from leading Pembroke citizens, but the damage had already been done.

I worked on the base in Petawawa when the Airborne first came here in the 1970s and the general feeling at the time was that moving the regiment here was a political move—not one wanted by the Airborne or by this base.

However, when they did arrive, they impressed many people from day one. They were the only unit that I can recall wearing distinctively marked T-shirts, and to everyone's amazement the wives and children wore them too! We had never seen anything like that here before. They were a group like no other, fiercely loyal and very protective of each other—a distinct, close family. Emotions from others that started out as resentment soon turned to admiration and envy. Before long, other units began sporting their own unit T-shirts on base.

It was about this time that I began to pay closer attention to the media reports in the local paper. I was appalled at how unfair their reports were and how prejudiced they were against the Airborne and the base as well. Whether it was a traffic violation by a service member or a fight at a local bar, if military were involved it made headlines.

Many times over the years I have seen the military called in to assist during civilian disasters. One has only to think of the bridge here in Petawawa on Old Highway 17 collapsing—the military engineers erected a Bailey bridge as a temporary measure until the community could arrange to have a replacement made. I remember, years ago, when the engineers were called in yet again to help search for a scientist missing in the woods in Quebec. In Renous, New Brunswick, a bridge was also built by the engineers when the existing one collapsed.

I am sure everyone reading this book can think back and recall one incident when the military 'came to the rescue.' It seems that we are nice to have around when there is a civil disaster, but other than that we are fair game for any criticism civilians feel erroneously justified in throwing our way.

However, those were the days of 'us' and 'them,' and both the civilian and military communities have tried very hard in the ensuing years to bridge that gap in every way possible. While I don't think we are there yet, great strides have been made, and with the military's open policy in effect, let's hope that there won't be a necessity for a bridge over the gap between military and civilians, but just one long smooth highway.

I must mention here that my husband was never in the Canadian Airborne Regiment, but having worked on this base for many, many years I definitely feel the Airborne as a whole have been unfairly treated as a result of the Somalia incidents. At the time of this writing, the scheduled courts-martial have not reached their conclusion. But regardless of their outcome, the wives and children do not deserve to be treated any differently than anyone else.

To all members of The Canadian Airborne Regiment: hold your heads up high, wear your maroon berets and T-shirts with dignity and pride.

Yugoslavia
Fond Farewells

I said goodbye to my brother today,
He's gone overseas so far away.
He's my brother, my friend, he helps me along,
When I'm down, he's up, when I'm weak, he's strong.
Although I need him as always before,

In Yugoslavia they need him more.
With the UN and the International Police,
He's supposed to be there to keep the peace.
The idea doesn't sound so bad,
Except there's not much peace to be had.
They've got blankets and food and supplies galore,
Needed so badly because of the war.

Winter will be here very soon now,
I'm warm in my home wondering how
I can help these people so badly in need,
Of relief from all this hatred and greed.
I feel for the children so hungry and cold,
They've lost their homes and families I'm told.

So I'll lend them my brother to help them too,
He's precious to me so it's not easy to do.
Seeing him go where there's danger and grief,
To do his job and protect our beliefs.
I'll see him when he comes home,
But I pray for the sisters there
Who said goodbye to their brothers today.

—Leanne Derrah
For her brother Sgt Grant Gervais (1st Battalion,
The Royal Canadian Regiment), who was
serving in the former Yugoslavia.

The following is another example of how families draw together in upsetting times, and how important the lines of communication must be:

Listening to the news and possible further UN taskings for the Canadian military, I sat down with my 14-year-old daughter and asked her if she knew what might happen if her Father had to go on another UN tour. She said yes she did understand, that it was his job and he would have to go, but she also knew from our experience with the Persian Gulf, that as a family we would still survive. It would be rough, but we ARE a family and we would be OK.

Reactions to the news that their husbands really were going to the former Yugoslavia varied, but the following comments are representative:

Shocked, hurt, worried, afraid I might lose him. Scared to be alone in a new town.

Please leave fast so you will come back fast. I hate the waiting period!

Surprised! Their tour, duties, travel and purpose were questionable at the time of departure and we both expected the whole thing to be cancelled before leaving.

A realization that it was his job which he has trained for all along. Also, a sense of panic in that we only had two weeks to unpack our furniture and effects from Europe and get settled.

Happy for him and supportive.

Numbness at first, then depression, then acceptance.

Anxiety of the challenge ahead—the challenge of being apart, being a single parent, of being totally responsible for everything.

One of my biggest fears for the future is my husband dying. It's hard to explain, but I think it's partly because my parents are in their 70s and I worry about losing them. They are just so helpful to us, it's hard to imagine life without them. And I worry about my husband being taken away from me.

I worry that he is going to stray (from the area they are supposed to stay in) out of curiosity and that something will happen to him.

The second largest fear after their husband's safety was always present but often remained unspoken—as if by not talking about it maybe it wouldn't happen. "What if he shoots someone? How will he feel? How will I feel about him? How will I tell the children?" Equally important were other fears that perhaps many wives were dealing with for the first time:

What will I do if I get sick? Our family is in Nova Scotia—who will take the baby?

Will I be able to go through to the end—sane?

Will I be a good enough, patient parent?

Will he be different when he returns?

What if the children's behaviour changes for the worse?

How will I deal with the kids missing their father?

Will we both survive this ordeal? Some days I wonder if I will need therapy. Who knows?

This time there was no denying the fact that danger was not far away. News reports of a local soldier being killed in Yugoslavia set everyone's already irregular heartbeat going full tilt—waiting for word on who it was. Relief at finding out that it is 'not my husband' was immediately replaced with anguish for the family of the dead soldier.

Apprehension was high on this tasking, and those waiting for their husbands to return on leave had already endured a long, long wait. "Is he OK?"; "Will he be able to get home for his holiday so I can see him and touch him and know that he really is OK?"; "When will it all end?"; "How is he holding up under all of this?"

Anxieties run high, along with the knowledge that if he does make it home on leave, "We are going to have to say goodbye again and this time it's going to be ten times harder . . ." In fact, not all holiday reunions are as successful as was hoped. Some husbands and wives feel no one could possibly understand what each had been dealing with and oftentimes the expectations for a completely harmonious reunion are set far too high. "It's impossible to make up for a several months' separation in one or two weeks."

✻ ✻ ✻

It's the end of November and with my husband in Yugoslavia, it is just sinking in with the girls that Dad will not be here for Christmas. Of course the usual question comes up: "Why does my Dad have to be away?" I try to look on the positive side of things and tell them what an important job their Dad is doing for the poor children in the war-torn country. I try to show them how lucky we are—but they are young and it is hard for them to understand.

When he left for Yugoslavia, I drove him to the unit headquarters. Instead of stopping at the main entrance, he had me stop at the entrance on the opposite side of the building and said he would get out there. So we said our goodbyes and then I watched him. The door was locked so he had to walk to the main entrance. I think he knew all along it would be locked, but just needed that time alone to compose himself before facing all the others. It's not an easy time for any of us. But the military is his life, it is what he has always wanted to do. [During the course of this interview, we stopped for a few minutes as her 10-year-old daughter was crying in her bedroom. Having just moved to Petawawa this past summer she was really missing some of her friends. When her mother went to see what was wrong, she found pictures of her friends and her father all over the bed. Her daughter cried how much she missed her father and again the question surfaced, "Why does *my* Dad have to be away?" After consoling her daughter and sharing a few chuckles on recalling some funny incidents, the bad time passed and her daughter was able to finish writing to her friends.]

When he first got to Yugoslavia he told me he found it exhilarating and I knew he would because he loves the military lifestyle so much. Is this tour going to change him? I know he is affected by the condition of the children he sees. He was

throwing chocolate bars to the kids as they passed in the truck, but had to stop that as the CO felt it was wrong to show favoritism. I had just bought some candies shaped like Santa, etc. to send to him for the children, but I guess now he won't be able to give them out.

When my husband goes on a six-month tour it usually takes another six months before our relationship is back to where we both want it. There is the apprehension before he leaves—we want to enjoy what time we have left together, but knowing that he is going to be gone for such a long time always seems to creep into our thoughts. His actual departure for the six months is extremely difficult for both of us, but by the time he has returned, I have established a routine that suits me and I have managed on my own and here is THIS PERSON coming back into my life. I have to step aside and make room for him—as the father of my kids, as the disciplinarian, as the maker of decisions. This can be a rough time and takes a while to adjust to. So it's about a year of the emotional yo-yo before things settle down to 'normal.' But once that has been accomplished, then you are no doubt facing his going away again!

Home Fires Burning

What distinguishes most military wives is that despite the hardships they endure, they understand the importance of their role.

One thing these UN taskings have taught me is that no matter how difficult we wives find this lifestyle at times, all we have to do is look at the reason our husbands are required to go to these war-torn countries and we see some of the problems people there are dealing with every day. It makes our complaining so insignificant.

The minute the guys are home you forget all the bad things that happened. It's like having a child—once it has been born you don't remember all the pain you went through until the next time...

❋　❋　❋

We lived in Germany when we were first married and I used to have nightmares about WW III breaking out and I would tell my husband jokingly that if it happened, I would break both his legs so he couldn't go to war and he said it wouldn't do any good as they would send him anyway! It was an exaggeration on both our parts, of course, but I guess he was trying to tell me that if there was another war it was his job to go ...

❋　❋　❋

My husband has been gone for three months this time, and yes, I miss him terribly. However, I do have my own routine, and I know when he comes home there is going to be that potpourri of emotions to deal with again. The joy of seeing him again, the resentment of his stepping into my organized life, dealing with the little nit-picky things about him that always bothered me but that I have not had to contend with for three months. I love the man more than life itself, but this man will come home and disrupt the life the children and I have made for ourselves. Life as a military wife is an emotional roller coaster. However, we have reached the stage in our relationship which is a very close and loving one, that when he telephones and we talk about his return, we can joke about all the emotions we will both be dealing with on his return. At last we know what those emotions are and why we go through them—that's more than half the battle. Once you recognize these emotions for what they are and have reached acceptance of the turmoil you are going to experience every time that special man 'comes and goes,' then you can go through the process, just let it happen and then move on from there . . .

A plethora of emotions are experienced by all the wives when their partner arrives home safely after his UN tour. Naturally there is relief, thankfulness and joy, but there is also apprehension and the need for understanding. It's a time to once again try to settle into being a 'complete family.' It's a time for re-acquainting and re-adjusting. A time to realize that to pick up exactly where you left off when he went away is unrealistic, as both of you have changed during this time apart. Realizing that these recent UN taskings are like no other and that your husband will need time to come to terms with all that he has seen and accomplished in that war-torn country, the wise military wife will give him the time he needs to adjust. Eventually the nightmares will become less frequent and less intense. Each and every soldier must deal with his tour in his own way, and whether he opens up and talks to you of his fears and concerns or feels it's necessary to 'go it alone' in dealing with his emotions, be there for him. He needs you now more than ever.

Chapter 11

Is the Other Side of the Fence Painted?

Retirement! That time when both Private John Doe and General John Doe become just plain Mister Doe. An adjustment? Definitely—but not only for him—for his wife and family as well.

For some, retiring and adjusting to civilian life runs as smoothly as a new coat of paint on the other side of the fence. For others, that side of the fence isn't even painted!

❈   ❈   ❈

While some families are more prepared than others, it's a move like no other. When your husband decides to 'pull the pin' and leave his uniforms behind, life suddenly takes on a whole new set of emotions.

For those who make this important decision together, things run much more smoothly than for those service members who see retirement as an individual effort. However, whichever group you belong to, retirement can be a very emotional time. You are leaving the cocoon of the military family and flying off on your own. Gone is the support network, the closeness of mess life, the constant meeting up again with old friends from posting to posting. In its place can be found the eagerness to take on this new venture or the dread of adjusting to civilian life. Here's how some wives feel about retirement:

My husband was thinking of getting out once he had his 20 years in and that really scared me. The military life is all I know, as my Dad was military too and the thought of staying in one place 'forever' is just awful. However, he did change his mind and I can remember the tremendous relief I felt. I don't know how I am going to handle it when he does retire.

It was hard moving to a civilian community because most of the people have lived in the same area all their lives and don't have that much to talk about. You can't talk to them about politics as they don't know much outside of their own area. You can't talk to them about Quebec because it's so foreign to them. I want to make friends with the wives but it's hard because right now the most important thing to them is the sewer system they are putting in down the road. There is nothing wrong with that, it's just that our lives have been so different and their world seems so small compared to mine.

Retirement! It's not quitting a job, it's a change of lifestyle. And when? They are too young to totally retire, too old for a new career or to be considered for hiring. If they retire earlier, they are penalized by a cut in their pensions. I also think the military leaves them in the dark by doing too many things for the guys, thus training them to be dependent. How are our husbands supposed to become independent civilians at the age of 55 or earlier when someone (the Army) tells them for 30 years what underwear to wear! No wonder so many guys hang on year after year despite how fed up they are. But it's the wife and kids that suffer.

My time in the military atmosphere was an adventure. It was a good life and I did miss it at first. I missed the social times, but I've adjusted now.

After 33 years of putting the military first at the expense of me and the family, many times when it wasn't necessary, he finally wondered what for! The system really doesn't care about you when you retire—you're forgotten as soon as you're out the door.

My husband had just finished his six-month tour in the Golan and had been home for about 8 or 9 months when he was posted to Toronto. He had less than a year left before retirement. We certainly did not want to move as we were in our retirement home. So it meant that he would go unaccompanied for that year. We were just recovering from the last long separation and here we were, having to deal with another separation even longer! My husband asked to have the posting changed as we had always heard you're supposed to get your choice for a final posting—so they sent him back to the Golan for another six months!! It seems that so many men who are near retirement receive terrible postings that they definitely do not want. It almost seems like Ottawa does it deliberately hoping the guys will refuse and be forced to take an early retirement which means they take a penalty on their pension. That's some thank you for giving the military your 'all' for most of your adult life!

Retirement means no more moving! The security is gone but I look forward to it—you'll know exactly what is going to happen each day and year and I think this will be more of an adventure!

When my husband celebrated his 25th anniversary in the Forces, we had a surprise party for him, the first one ever. It was an accomplishment for many reasons, but during the evening, without giving it any thought beforehand, I suddenly said to him, "The first 25 years were for you and the next 25 years are for me!" I think my comments surprised us both, but when you think about it, why not? After the sacrificing, loneliness, etc., that we deal with, retirement should be a time for husbands to try and make up for the lost time apart, for regaining the closeness that might have stretched somewhat after all the years of many separations.

We have lived in the same community now for about 10 years, which is quite a feat for us, as we were used to moving about every three years. This is the best time of our lives. I like going to local shops and being greeted by my name and not feeling that I am just another face in the crowd. I like feeling part of a community and being able to contribute to that community. I guess I feel it's time for me to pay back with my time and efforts for all the years when it wasn't possible to do so. This area is no doubt where our children will settle and it has become 'home' to all of us. We have finally grown roots and it's wonderful!

Togetherness

However, retirement is certainly an adjustment time, and for those wives who are used to their husbands being away for long periods of time, 'togetherness' can take some getting used to.

After 25 years of seeing my husband continually away year in and year out the 'togetherness' of retirement took some adjusting for both of us. We used to talk about retirement and joke that we didn't know if we could stand each other for 24 hours a day!!

I was so used to having some quiet time to myself over the years —which I treasured! When I was alone so much, handling all the responsibilities, these quiet times 'just for me' helped me keep my sanity. I am still working, so my husband has his 'quiet time' all day, every day, Monday to Friday. It's hard for him to understand my need to be alone from time to time—it took me a while to understand it myself.

I didn't realize what was missing from my life when he first retired until the first time he went away (hunting) and suddenly my world felt 'normal' again!

When we were first married I'd get so upset every time he went away and I cried just as much the last time as I did the first time. So who would have thought after all these years of 'wishing' we'd be together more that now I'm 'wishing' for some time alone! However, it's been a few years of 'togetherness' now and we're still talking to each other so I guess that's a good sign!

❈　　❈　　❈

At first it was great having him home continually after so many years apart. But after a while, I thought I'd go nuts! Every time I turned around he was there. I just wasn't used to that. It's like wishing and wishing for something and then when you get it, it's not just what you thought it was!

❈　　❈　　❈

My husband is a senior officer in a high profile position. He will be retiring soon and moving right into a civilian high profile job. When will there be time for him? When will there be time for us? He just doesn't understand that I don't enjoy the same enthusiasm for his work that he does . . .

A while ago we attended a retirement dinner for a military friend. I couldn't help but reflect on just what that retirement meant. Although the get-together was a happy occasion, with many friends sharing in the event, I wondered if it was also a sad time. Many military men have spent their whole adult life in one job, serving their country, and all of a sudden that comes to an end and a new adventure is to take its place. I suspect the feeling for some must be similar to leaving home for the first time. You are letting go of a secure life and facing the unknown. Pretty scary at any age.

Life takes us through many ups and downs as well as many stages, but retiring from the military is a major event which requires a lot of understanding from the whole family.

About 12 years ago I attended a mixed happy hour at my husband's mess. I met him at the mess after work and, arriving earlier than most wives, I sat back and just observed those around me. I don't think it was until that particular event that I realized just how much of a 'family' they really are. The closeness they share not only in their daily work, but in their personal lives as well, is something that you don't see in civilian corporations. There is a bonding there that's evident in the way the guys related to each other.

I know it's difficult for wives at times—we complain about how much the job takes hubby away from home, and then of course there are the happy hours and get-togethers the guys have after an exercise, etc. Yes, sometimes we do feel left out, but that night I saw something for the first time. I began to slowly understand what this close-knit group was all about! So, when retirment time comes, many are not only letting go of the only job they ever had, they are letting go of a particular lifestyle, and moving outside the 'family.'

Whose Retirement Is It?

When my husband retired, he had the choice of a candlelight dinner where his co-workers and military friends and their wives would gather for a farewell evening, or a military luncheon for just the men. He chose the luncheon. While I could understand his decision, I must say that I was really disappointed and hurt. Yes, I know he was the one retiring, but in a way I felt I was retiring too. I had to adjust to a new lifestyle apart from the military life and functions, and there was no opportunity for me to 'say goodbye.' I don't think he even thought to include me in his decision. I had hoped we could 'retire' as a family, with our children (who were then adults in their 20s) attending to see just how their father's military friends said goodbye to him, and for once show them what military functions are all about. However, it certainly ended up 'his' retirement, and I still feel that I was left out.

Scan Seminars

The military has established a Second Career Assistance Network (SCAN) to make the transition to civilian life easier. SCAN seminars are held periodically on each military base and are open to service members with five years or less remaining before their retirement from the military. With the recent introduction of the Forces Reduction Plan (FRP), special seminars have been established for those personnel leaving the military under this plan. At all of these seminars many subjects are presented—financial planning, real estate, a review of the procedures to follow when it becomes time to initiate the paperwork necessary to retire, talks by retired personnel on what the 'real world' is really like, and what to expect in the way of a financial settlement when you do retire.

Wives are encouraged to attend these seminars, yet so few do. Granted, some wives are working and not able to take time off, but if my survey results are accurate, the majority of military wives handle the family finances. Why then are they not making an extra effort to attend these seminars when they are about to make one of the major decisions of their lives? Part of the answer lies with the men—some believe that it is *their* retirement and has nothing to do with their wives. I suspect there are many wives out there who were not even aware that the seminars were being held or that their husbands were attending! You are wrong, men, your retirement has everything to do with your wives. Who is the lady who has packed up and moved with you from Timbuktu to Ottawa and everywhere else all these years? Here you are about to decide on perhaps the final move of you life. Surely this lady who has given up so much over the years for you and your career is entitled to some consideration on this final move. *You owe it to her!*

Before my husband retired, we attended a SCAN seminar. Because he was being medically released as opposed to retiring, I was worried about how we would manage and just what all had to be done when retirement time came. As the realities of life after the military were explained to us, I tried to absorb all that was being said and relate it to our situation. It really was a scary feeling for me to finally have to come to terms with the fact that our 'time' had definitely come.

One seminar speaker, Marv Rabjohn, caused a ray of sunshine to penetrate through all this heavy thinking. I found myself not only sitting up and paying full attention, but feeling the tension slowly ease. I listened to him talk of living on his Sergeant's pension and how he and his wife had perfected use of the barter system. Despite his limited income, this man did not have the word 'stress' in his personal dictionary. He was the most laid-back, happy, contented individual I have ever met! And because of his calm, cool manner and the confidence with which he spoke, I left the seminar with a different feeling than when I entered. I knew that whatever life held for us 'after the military' we would manage, we would be OK.

Marv had shown us the other side of the 'coin of retirement.' If you are not hung up on material possessions, you can have a life without mega funds—it all boils down to expectations and priorities and what is really important to you. As he explained, his lifestyle compromises between the necessity of earning a living and living itself. How you reach that balance is up to you.

Later I had the opportunity to spend some time with Marv and his wife Bunny. I wanted to know how they survived. He retired as an Airforce Sergeant in 1981, at age 45, with a pension of $550 per month. "I knew when I retired from the military I really wanted to retire. I did not want to go from one job to another. A few years before retirement I purchased two acres from my father and we bought a modular home. It's a quiet rural area. We grow all our own vegetables." (Their home, surrounded by flowers of every description, two vegetable garden areas and a well-manicured lawn, is lovely!)

Bunny admitted their lifestyle took some getting used to, and in the beginning she was more sceptical about its success than her husband. "When we came here I didn't know how to garden. I read up on it and taught myself. I do a lot of preserving of jams, jellies and pickles."

Before Marv retired, he studied everything he could get his hands on about the economy. Over 12 years ago, he predicted the present recession.

Marv's philosophy is quite simple. If you want something, take the dollar value of that item divided by an average hourly wage and you'll come up with how many hours you would have to work to pay for it. Then decide if the item is a 'need' or a 'want' and go from there. Decide whether you really want to work that many hours just to have that particular item. It's all a matter of priorities.

Keeping in mind that his aim was to enjoy life while he was young and healthy enough, here are some of the bartered items he has been successful at:

"I had this friend that had a restaurant. He had an older car for sale so we made a deal for so many apple pies (the restaurant owner tested the first pie) in exchange for the car. Bunny baked the pies."

At one point a Honda was traded for a wall unit and then that was traded for a load of wood.

Bunny's comments:

"We used to go to the farmer's market a few years ago. I would make chelsea buns and we would sell some of our vegetables.

"Another friend sells corn stoves. Marv would go to the fall fairs to help sell these stoves. He'd also help the owner on his farm with the animals and he'd feed the animals when his friend was away. In exchange for this help he would get a side of beef.

"He receives an honorarium for speaking at SCAN seminars, which he has done for over eight years. He also does payrolls on his home computer (which he got in exchange for something else) for a few small companies in the area.

"I got a free checkup at the dentist and we supply him with tomatoes all season.

"Marv bartered for an irrigation system for our garden. He worked for a man who had a tree service business and garden centre. He helped him out for a while for no salary and then one day the man asked him what he wanted in return for his help, and he got his irrigation system.

"Sometimes we go to the Salvation Army Clothing Depot. At one point Marv needed a suit for a wedding. If a suit cost $300 it would take many hours of work to pay for it. If you can buy one for $10 you only have to work for one hour to pay for it. And that's what he did. Later on we went back to the Depot and got a London Fog topcoat to match for next to nothing!

"I clean my father-in-law's house next door and I am paid by the Veteran's Association.

"I get free hair cuts. My friend and I do each other's hair.

"Marv's philosophy is simple—no salary, no deductions, no taxes. He is exactly where he wants to be. We are free to do whatever we want to do. We have no need for cheques or a chequing account, so we save on all the associated service charges. Some of our friends have heard my husband talk at seminars and they say 'more power to you.' My family thought it was a little strange. They thought he was too young to retire. But he did his time and wanted something different. Now he can pick and choose what he wants to do. Our sons thought our choice of a lifestyle a little unusual, but they are used to it now."

However, both Marv and Bunny admitted that their lifestyle is not for everyone. "You need to be a person who is not afraid to take chances, who can barter for what he wants rather than just pay the price being asked. You also need to be somewhat outgoing and able to talk to people."

Food for thought? Sure is. Whether you agree with his principles, or whether you think his lifestyle is not for you, it is another alternative to consider when leaving the military atmosphere. I thoroughly enjoyed my visit with this very hospitable couple. I envied them their gardens, their home, their lifestyle and above all their 'stress-free' lives. Perhaps, the barter system is the key to living longer . . .

Recognition

One Commanding Officer's wife had both foresight and a genuine interest in the important role each wife made to her husband's career. She designed a 'Retirement Certificate,' which was presented at an appropri-

ate occasion to each wife when her husband was celebrating his retirement. How I would have appreciated receiving something like that—
something that I could hang on the wall for all to see, something that
recognized my 'career' as a military wife! A gift to be treasured always.
Women are a sentimental lot and it's the little, thoughtful things that
make us happy. Being appreciated is at the top of the list.

Chapter 12

60 Years as an RCR Wife

In closing, I offer the following condensation of comments written by Lila Ina (Titus) Hovey. A very gracious lady 84 years young, Lila wrote an account of her entire adult life in 1992 and titled it "60 Years as an RCR Wife."

With the trials and tribulations we go through as military wives and how 'hard done by' we sometimes feel we are, there is much cause for reflection in Lila's writings. The saying "There is always someone worse off" is so true and perhaps this saying is something that should be prominently displayed on every fridge door as a daily reminder of just how lucky we really and truly are. Throughout Lila's story you will see that despite the different timeframe in which she spent her military life, many similarities remain today and probably always will with this lifestyle—the agony of

separations, the joy of homecomings, the constant moving, the illnesses and tragedies handled alone, the career disappointments and the 'making do.' Just as timeless are the closeness of good friends, the travels and mess life, the opportunity to create our own independence and, above all, the great motivation to make the most of what life offers.

Lila (from Sussex, New Brunswick) met her future husband Bert in 1930. In 1931 he joined The RCR as a Pte and left for Aldershot Camp in Nova Scotia and then on to their barracks in the Citadel in Halifax. Their romance was conducted by mail with an occasional weekend and an annual leave of 21 days. "In those days there was an Army regulation that stated regardless of rank, a soldier had to have six years service and be 26 years of age before he could get permission to marry, and his girlfriend had to produce two recommendations from prominent citizens to say she was suitable to be a wife in the Permanent Force, officers included. That was no problem for me. I got one from our Minister and one from our family Doctor." Bert had the service but not the age, so they married quietly in Saint John, New Brunswick. When Bert reached 26 years they were married again and officially recognized by the Army as a married couple. He then received permission to live at home, returning to barracks each morning. Now that they were officially recognized, they were able to receive 'rations.'

Once each week we sat making out our ration list for delivery by horse transport. The only meat we ever ordered was slabs of bacon, ham or back bacon. If for some reason you drew 'ration allowance' you got fifty cents a day. If you drew 'rations in kind' they came at wholesale prices and the average was about thirty-two cents a day. We got milk tickets and bread tickets. I could manage quite a meal on these rations. I had been well taught by my mother!

In 1937 Lila and Bert shared a housing unit in the Hydrastone district in north-end Halifax with another military couple. "The rent was $25 a month, so we paid $12 and they paid $13. They had a kitchenette and a coal burning kitchen stove. We had two rooms and a hall and we shared the bathroom. We took turns buying and stoking the hard coal or coke for the furnace during the cold weather."

At a time when some couples were using orange crates and second-hand furniture, Lila and Bert scrimped and saved and shopped carefully.

Bert built kitchen cupboards and they were able to buy a new dining room set, had $200 in the bank and no debts! Their next ambition was to have a home of their own and after much searching, they bought a building lot for $50, which Bert called "a rock pile with some bushes growing on it." A contractor was talked into building a one-bedroom bungalow and it sat on nine cement posts which eventually were incorporated into a foundation and basement.

By now it was early summer of 1939. Bert went to Aldershot to summer camp and I went back home to Saint John, New Brunswick. By the end of the summer the war clouds were hanging over us, especially The Royal Canadian Regiment and other permanent force units. We lived in our new home for about two weeks. Bert was on call night and day. We didn't have much choice but to close up our new home and say goodbye to our dreams. We put our furniture in storage and I lived in two rooms near the barracks.

From there they moved to London, Ontario and on to Valcartier, Quebec. Next came word that The RCR were going overseas. Lila returned to Halifax and from Bert's letters (he was in Quebec City) she knew The Regiment would soon be in Halifax on their way to the British Isles.

Through an army friend, Lila knew what day The Regiment would arrive at the Immigration Sheds.

I spent hours around that area, trying to get in. Finally, the chap on the gate said 'You are one very insistent lady,' and let me in. Around about this time we got word that there had been a train accident and that maybe one of the men had been killed. He turned out to be the first RCR casualty of the war. When they came in, I saw an NCO that I knew and he said 'Bert is OK. He is back there somewhere,' and pretty soon he appeared, leading the 65 men that he had in his platoon, including reinforcements.

We spent a couple of hours together. What an experience! Some marriages took place and some were consummated right there in the Immigration Sheds. One I will never forget—a young couple were married. The girl must have been about 15 and the boy not too much older. That boy never came back. Finally the time had arrived. Bert was the WO that gave the command 'A Coy pick up your kit, sling arms, right turn and follow me.' I stood back in the crowd waving goodbye. It was our second wedding anniversary, 18 December 1939.

For some unknown reason, I didn't leave right away. I guess I thought they just might get off the ship again, and sure enough, once they found their place aboard ship, they came back ashore and we had another hour or so together, and then our final goodbyes. We didn't know for how long, but in my case it was for three and a half years . . .

Lila then decided to go back home in time for Christmas.

I was the only one in our family to have a loved one off to fight a war. There were 17 of us at home for Christmas dinner. The turkey was well basted with my tears—tears that I tried so hard to hide from the rest of the family. What a horrible feeling!

My husband and I numbered our letters and I sent a parcel twice each month. I numbered them too. They all got there and only one was any the worse for their long journey. The letters would come in bunches, three or four one day and another three or four a few days later, and then nothing for a while, all depending on the transatlantic shipping. I would write two or three letters each week. It was lonely, especially not knowing what the future might have to offer. You just carried on from day to day. I was always very sure that my husband would be home some day. Maybe my great faith helped him through.

During the next three and a half years Lila spent a great deal of time with relatives, friends and church groups and helping out in the family bakery (bread was 9-10 cents a loaf, gingersnaps were 25 cents for three dozen, pies 25 cents each).

In one letter from Bert he mentioned that eggs were very hard to come by in England so Lila sent some packed in a box of salt, and some packed in oatmeal.

One time Bert was out on a scheme and all he had to eat that day was a sandwich made from what they called black bread and one of my eggs, scrambled. I also sent cans of stew. He told me one cold rainy day they were out on a long route march. He spotted a cow lying in a pasture, chased her away, and he and two Sergeants that I knew sat on the now vacated warm spot to eat one of my cans of cold stew, using their bayonets to fish it out of the can! Bert used the oatmeal to make porridge for a late night snack.

One day a letter arrived from Bert, who was dealing with mixed feelings. By now he was Senior Company Sergeant Major of his unit and had his heart set on becoming Regimental Sergeant Major. However, someone else was appointed to the position. Bert then decided to become an officer. He expected the course to be in England but then wrote that it would be in Brockville, Ontario.

Finally a telegram arrived from Bert in Halifax telling me he was on his way to me. When the doorbell rang, I almost fell headlong down the stairs. There stood my Bert after an absence of three and a half years. I fell into his arms, so thankful that my husband was home again. That was April 1943.

After he had been gone so long Lila was not about to let Bert out of her sight again, so she travelled with him to Brockville (the only female aboard a special train car full of officer cadets). Once there, Lila was left at the train station to make her own way as Bert had to proceed with the others to the Training Centre. She had previously been told of a Hospitality House that helped young wives find a place to stay while their husbands were on course. Through them she found some rooms in an elderly couple's home, where she and Bert stayed for the next eighteen months.

Now came what I had feared the most. Bert was posted back overseas to The Regiment. Once again he took me home to my parents. Not long after he left to go overseas, I discovered that I was expecting our first child. Telegrams were unsatisfactory, so I wrote an airmail letter to tell him he was about to become a Daddy. We were both very pleased to know about this. The

airmail was a long time getting to him, and in April 1945 our
son was born prematurely and lived only a few hours.

Now another airmail followed Bert up the reinforcement stream and
caught up with him just as they were preparing to go into the last RCR
battle of World War II.

For some strange reason, I felt that if our baby was OK, Bert
would not be coming home, but if by some chance something
went wrong, as it did, then I was sure that he would be home.
As badly as I felt, this thought was there to comfort me . . .

One day I received a letter from Ijmuiden, Holland saying
Bert was coming home again. He arrived in Saint John 17
July 1945. My brother and his wife took me to the train station
to meet him. The station was roped off and we stood next to
the ropes. Suddenly I looked up and there he was. He had
climbed up a ladder on the baggage car and was looking over
the heads of the crowds looking for me. He signalled me to
stay put and he would come to the spot where I was standing.
It was great to be back together again. I thought the war days
were over, but not so . . .

My husband didn't tell me until the end of his leave that he
had volunteered for the Pacific Force. That was hard to take.
He would be leaving for another war, this time in the Pacific,
and that right soon. On the evening before the last day of his
leave, somebody dropped a bomb on Hiroshima. Bert was out
in my brother's workshop making hangers for his wardrobe
trunk. I dashed out and called him in. I said, 'The war is over.
Everybody is going down to the city square to celebrate, let's
get going!' He said 'Not me, I've seen all the mob scenes I
want to see.' He went back to his hangers.

The next day Bert went to the Depot in Fredericton for
further posting instructions. This time he got posted to
Debert, Nova Scotia, where he became second-in-command
of a company of the Carleton and York Regiment. They knew
the fighting was over, but they expected to become an Army of
Occupation as part of an American Force. After about a
month in Debert, the Pacific Force folded and Bert was post-
ed to the Sussex Sortation Centre as second-in-command of

the Administrative Wing. And here we were right back in the old home town, where we had started, back in 1930. Here we set up our first postwar home after waiting for six years to do so.

While I was trying to make up my mind what to do next, along came yet another posting. This time it was back to The RCR in Brockville.

In his role as Assistant Adjutant, Bert was the officer who got the names of all the officers as they were accepted or rejected for the postwar army. One day a message arrived with his name on it. It said, 'Authority is granted for this officer to resign his commission and he will be signed on as an Other Rank the following day.'

After several sleepless nights, Bert applied and was accepted as a student at the Veterinary College in Guelph. Then a senior officer from Ottawa HQ told the Adjt that there was a job waiting for Bert as a Warrant Officer Class II in Fredericton. All he had to do was ask for it. Now what do we do? If he got out and went to college he would be forfeiting 15 years service and it took only 20 to qualify for a pension.

When my husband was rejected from commissioned service after all we had been through, it came as a bitter disappointment to both of us. I asked who had been accepted, and when I heard some of the names, I could hardly believe what I was hearing. One in particular had been confirmed in the rank of Captain and accepted. He had fought his whole war in the comforts of Canada and had never seen a shot fired, except on the rifle range. But that is life, and we had to get on with it.

To get back to life in Brockville for a moment—we were there that second time for about eight months and by now we were expecting our second child. We had made several good friends among the Brockville people during our two tours of duty there. We attended church and often went to Brockville homes for a sing-song and nearly always a nice lunch. But now it was time to move on.

Bert took me back to my parents' place in Saint John once more, and went to his new posting with the Carleton and York Regiment in Fredericton. Places to live, be it rent or board,

*were scarce after the war. My doctor was a child specialist in
Saint John, so we felt that it was the best place for me to be
until our baby was born, especially after what had happened
the last time. I had an uncle living in Fredericton and Bert got
a room with them.*

*My husband put an ad in the Fredericton paper that said
"Wanted for cash—small house in Fredericton or Devon." He
got one answer. It came from an elderly lady who said she
would only sell to a returned veteran. We paid cash and
bought it. It needed a lot of work. No plumbing and no
electricity . . .*

Together Lila and Bert worked on their home, digging a cesspool,
building kitchen cupboards, painting, wallpapering, converting a large
hall into a nursery and building a bathroom. During this time their son
Walter flourished—playing happily away nearby in his playpen, sporting
clothes that Lila had made for him.

*Bert saw an ad in the paper offering an old sewing machine
for sale. He bought it thinking he would make it into a jigsaw,
but when I got one look at it that all changed.   I made about
half of our baby's clothes on it and did a lot more. He never
did get his jigsaw. Walter spent most of his summer days in his
carriage out on the veranda. Our neighbours used to stop and
talk to him. He knew the neighbours better than we did!*

*In May 1947 we bought our first car. We had tried to get a
Canadian car but none were available. Our Austin came from
England. Bert went over to Halifax and got it right off the
ship. Again, we paid cash—the whole sum of $1,800.*

In May 1948 they decided to buy a new home in a new housing project and rent their present home—their first venture into the real estate
market. Again they worked as a team, doing the landscaping and building a garage.

*I held the 2 x 4's and when we came to a part we didn't under-
stand, we went for a walk around the building area until we
found a garage at that stage of development.*

Lila put in a garden and was soon busy canning and preserving.

In the spring of 1950 Lila was not feeling well and was eventually admitted to the hospital in July of that year.

My parents came to be there while I was in the hospital. The day after I was admitted my mother suffered a cerebral haemorrhage. Mother was brought into the hospital and put in the room next to mine. I would go to her room 2 or 3 times a day and the doctor would send me back to bed. Four days later Mother passed away. I could hear them clearing her throat and then it stopped. Not a sound, but nobody came to my room to say a word. They were waiting for Bert and my doctor to come and tell me. The next day I found out I had a large cyst on one kidney and the kidney would have to be removed. Mother's funeral was to be in Saint John on Friday—I said, "Book me for Saturday!"

Lila wasn't allowed to attend her mother's funeral but Bert and Walter did, returning immediately afterwards to be with Lila during this time. In August 1951 Bert was posted to Korea but this was cancelled due to Lila's illness. However, he was posted to Camp Borden as an instructor, leaving Lila behind to pack up and sell the house. They traded their Austin for a Plymouth and made a bed for Lila in the back seat so that she could make the long trip. They eventually bought another house in Barrie and Bert was re-commissioned at the end of the first course.

In 1952 they again moved to Kingston, where Bert was posted in as a General Staff Officer Grade III at the Canadian Army Staff College. This time they bought another home that needed renovations. So once again 'the team' was in action.

Typically Army, before the kitchen cupboards were half finished, Bert was off to Borden to take a six weeks Lieutenant to Captain course. I continued on with the papering and painting. I don't know how we did it in such a short time. We even remodelled a bathroom.

By the summer of 1954 along came another posting. This time it was Canada's first ever Truce commission, and in about two weeks Bert was off half-way round the world, posted to Indochina. Believe me it was a queer feeling driving along the street behind an Army bus with my husband looking out the back window. My Dad was with us at the time and Bert asked him if he would stay with us until he returned, hopefully after an absence of about one year.

In April 1955 Lila again became very ill.

It was a very difficult task to convince External Affairs and military authorities that Bert should be brought home, but finally he got word and five days later he was home. He was not sure whether he would find me dead or alive. The diagnosis was not complete until a day or so later. They told him I had a poly-cystic liver and kidney (remember I only had one kidney). No malignancy, but there was nothing they could do for me. They sent me home. They told my husband that I had about five years to live. That was in 1955 and here I am writing these notes in 1992, some thirty years later! The ailment is still there, but I have learned how to cope with it.

Bert was then posted back to Kingston and retired from the regular Army in 1959 one day and was taken on strength at Queen's University Contingent Canadian Officers Training Corps (COTC) the next day as Training Officer. He had suffered a heart attack and so could not take on a regular job like most retirees did. In May he bought a magazine agency, which he ran from our home.

Lila's Dad spent his summers with them. In 1959 he was not feeling well and her brother thought it best for him to stay home in Saint John, but he still wanted to travel to Kingston.

On Aug 4, 1959 we met him in Windsor Station in Montreal. He died right there before our eyes a few minutes after we met him . . .

In May 1962 Lila again found herself in the hospital for a gall bladder operation, which necessitated five weeks in the hospital due to her previous problems.

In 1963 I was back again for yet another operation not quite so serious this time!

1966 saw more changes in our lives. That year Bert was promoted to Lieutenant Colonel and became Commanding Officer of the COTC Unit. In June 1968 we travelled to London to The RCR reunion. It was great, just meeting and remembering so many old friends.

In 1971 Bert started to teach Amateur Radio classes at night school at St. Lawrence College. He and his co-teacher wrote the Study Guides published by the Canadian Amateur Radio Federation. He did all the typing and illustrating, so I didn't see very much of him for about two years.

In 1973 Bert retired from his teaching job. He and Lila sold their home and moved into an apartment where they didn't have to worry about maintenance or snow removal. The years 1976 and 1978 saw more unhappy times for Lila, with the deaths of two of her brothers. In 1977 the official opening of KOTARA (Kingston Old Timers Amateur Radio Association) radio station was held. Bert was asked to head this group and Lila's role was to obtain all the furniture for the station and a lounge (at no cost to the Association!).

Back in 1979 our women's group in the church held a special evening and each one was asked to either model her own wedding dress or have somebody else do it for her. I was the only one in the whole group, at age 70, who could model the dress in which she had been married. The rest were all too big to get into their dresses! It was just a fun night.

Before going any further, I realize that I have said very little about Mess life. I have had experiences that might answer some questions in two ways. You see, I moved up from Corporal to Sergeants' Mess to the Officers' Mess, where I went from being the wife of a very junior member to that of a Lieutenant Colonel.

To start with, I was one of those few teetotalers. Some might think we were trying to be difficult, but not so. Moving up from the Sergeants' Mess to the Officers' Mess was a bit awesome at first. Again I wondered how I would be accepted, but now that I look back, some of my best years were spent in the Officers' Messes, from New Brunswick to Ontario.

Time after time when Bert was teaching and commanding young officers, I was asked by young girls, some of them brides, "What do I do in an Officers' Mess?" My answer was, and always has been, "Just be yourself. Don't act shy and don't try to impress. Just be yourself." Now, in my 80s, it still applies, and I often marvel at the respect that comes my way as the wife of a fairly senior officer and for just being me.

It was in 1982 that the Kingston and District Branch of The RCR Regimental Association was formed and my husband was elected to the office of branch President. The first event for the wives to attend was the Charter dinner. MGen Dan Spry was the senior guest. I had stood on the sidelines in the 1930s in Halifax when the Company NCOs (including my MCpl husband) formed an arch of bayonets for the senior guest's wedding (there were not enough officers to form the guard). That evening was the first time I had known his wife had to produce the same type of recommendations that I did, from two prominent citizens, before she could marry an RCR officer. Her family was a well-known Halifax business family. She was almost insulted!

In May 1983 Lila and Bert decided to move "one more time" and purchased a condo in Kingston.

We attended a Branch dinner in October 1983 at which we presented the Branch with a VRI Banner. I embroidered the date and our names down in one corner of the banner. Maybe someday it will be a reminder that this old couple was once part of The Regiment.

In 1985 Bert handed over his job as President of the Kingston and District Branch of The RCR Association to LCol Ian Hodson. Back in 1937, when we were married without permission, Ian's father, Major V. Hodson, was Officer Commanding Halifax Station, The RCR. We were greatly embarrassed one day walking along the street, Bert in uniform and both of us with an armful of groceries. Who should come around the corner but Major Hodson! The incident passed quickly, but there were soldiers in our position who were not re-engaged at the end of their three year term.

The year 1987 was the year of our 50th wedding anniversary. It was practically impossible to get suitable accommodations on December the 18th, the actual day. It was too close to Christmas. A group of friends engaged the big dining room at the Cataraqui Golf and Country Club for an October celebration instead. Friends and relatives came from New Brunswick, British Columbia and from different parts of Ontario. One couple came all the way up from Louisville, Kentucky to be there. Then later we went by train to Saint John in time for my sister-in-law and her daughter to hold an "at home" for us on December 18. More relatives and friends. This too was a memorable day.

In 1988 Lila's third brother died and she was the only one left of her family.

It is a strange feeling to be the only one left. I was the one they were all concerned about. I miss them but I have no regrets. I remember them all with love and affection.

June of that year saw Lila and Bert take a long car ride to London for another RCR reunion.

I think one of the things that stands out mostly was the evening of the retreat. It was cold and we were bundled up against the cold wind. One young RCR couple had brought along chairs and a blanket. They got up and insisted that we sit down while they wandered about watching the proceedings. That was so typical of the close association between the young and the old that I shall never forget it.

In June 1991 the executive of the Kingston and District Branch put on a dinner to celebrate my husband's 60 years as an RCR. They presented me with a dozen roses. They said it was 'for putting up with that old soldier for all these years.'

On reading this, one might say we have had a lot of separations and set-backs but we are both inclined to let the bad things slip and remember only the good things that happened . . .

Lila's best friend and husband Bert passed away in December 1992—one week before their 55th wedding anniversary. Two months later Lila fell and had to be hospitalized. However, she was soon back in her condo keeping in touch with her longstanding friends, accepting 'what is' and moving on from there. Of Bert she says she misses him terribly but they had a good life together and she will always remember the good times.

Lila, you are one special lady!

After reading Lila's full account of her life I thought I had just finished a best-selling love story! I felt the love that she and Bert shared. I agonized at the thought of their long separations and I cried envisioning their reunions. There is one very important message that I learned from her story. No matter what lifestyle you choose, if you and your mate work side by side and always think of each other before yourself, your marriage will succeed. Chimo!

Epilogue
Reflections and Predictions

What does the future hold for military wives? There are many new challenges these special women will have to deal with, and the strength they have shown in the past will definitely be necessary in the future. More wives will be working and establishing careers of their own. This will mean more 'commuting marriages' and fewer families moving as a unit. How will this affect the children? How will couples handle this added strain on their marriage?

With the reduction of Forces personnel, an added strain will be placed on service members, who might be called upon to participate in more than one UN Peacekeeping/Peacemaking tour. In addition, those remaining after cutbacks are faced with working harder for less— another added strain. Adding to the general frustration is the necessity of working with old, outdated equipment. How is this going to affect not only the individual, but the family unit as a whole? There are so many unanswered questions.

Today's military wives and those of the future must be emotionally stronger than ever, must ensure they are ready to meet the challenge this lifestyle demands and must continue to support each other and draw strength from that support. The men will have to meet the challenges of more taskings with fewer personnel and more time away from home. I have no doubt their wives will also meet the challenges facing them because, after all, they really are special.

So many women have asked me if I had to do it all over again would

I still choose to be a military wife. A difficult question to answer. I didn't really choose the lifestyle, I chose the *man* and the lifestyle was part and parcel of who he was. Did I enjoy the lifestyle? Yes and no. As I get older, the spark that ignited the challenge of seeing new places and experiencing life in different settings has gone out. In its place is the need to re-establish family ties, to spend more time with my relatives whom I have seen so little of during my adult life and to have my children spend more time getting to know their aunts, uncles and cousins (difficult when we are thousands of miles away).

I guess if we could all take the wisdom of maturity and transplant it into newlyweds, life could take us on many different paths. However, to honestly answer this question, I say yes! For me the advantages far outweighed the disadvantages. It's been a good, full life. Among other things the military lifestyle teaches you tolerance, independence and how to be resourceful, but like any marriage you have to constantly work at it. After all, isn't life really what *you* make of it?

About the Author

A secretary since the tender age of 17, Dianne's interest in writing grew from her many letters to friends and family while living in Germany, following her marriage there to a member of the Canadian Armed Forces. This interest was to expand as she and her family moved from coast to coast in Canada.

Although this is Dianne's first book, her writings are quite familiar to both military and civilian readers in the Petawawa/Pembroke area of Ontario. A few years ago Dianne was producing three weekly columns, two of which earned her the title of "The Erma Bombeck of Petawawa" and which appeared in the military newspaper *The Base Post* at Canadian Forces Base Petawawa and the local community paper, the *Pembroke Observer*. Her third column, which also appeared in the *Observer*, provided information and detailed events within the military community.

Dianne has worked for the military as a secretary for over 15 years, currently as the Commanding Officer's secretary at 1st Battalion, The Royal Canadian Regiment in Petawawa, Ontario. One of the founding members of the board of directors of CFB Petawawa's military family resource centre, Dianne also edited and produced the first-ever newsletter linking military family resource centres across Canada and Europe. *Hurry Up and Wait* was written with the interests of military wives uppermost in Dianne's mind. This concern continues with her column "Down Home Drivel," again in full swing in *The Base Post*, after its "leave of absence" to allow Dianne the time necessary to complete her book.

Dianne's career as a military wife spans over 26 years. She lives in Petawawa, Ontario, with her husband Warrant Officer (Ret'd) John L. Collier, a Field Engineer, and sons Chris and Trevor.

PHOTO: MICHAEL MONCION, PEMBROKE, ONTARIO

To order additional copies of
Hurry Up and Wait:
An inside look at life as a Canadian military wife
by Dianne Collier ($17.95)
or any of the other titles listed below, please state clearly what you
would like us to send you, with your name and address. Send your
order with payment for book(s) + shipping/handling* by cheque or
money order to :

Creative Bound Inc.
P.O. Box 424, 151 Tansley Drive
Carp, Ontario CANADA K0A 1L0

•Visa orders are also accepted by mail or fax at (613) 831-3643. Please
state your Visa number and expiry date.

•For bulk orders, please contact our office at tel. (613) 831-3641

*Shipping/handling, please add $3.00/book (to a maximum of $6.00)